翻译硕士(MTI)

汉英翻译技巧 12 讲

总策划 ◎ 翻译硕士考试研究中心

主编 ◎ 罗国强

中国政法大学出版社

2024·北京

图书在版编目（ＣＩＰ）数据

翻译硕士（MTI）汉英翻译技巧 12 讲/罗国强主编. —北京：中国政法大学出版社，2024.8
ISBN 978-7-5764-1356-4

Ⅰ. ①翻… Ⅱ. ①罗… Ⅲ. ①英语－翻译－研究生－入学考试－自学参考资料 Ⅳ. ①H315.9

中国国家版本馆 CIP 数据核字(2024)第 043697 号

出　版　者　　中国政法大学出版社

地　　　址　　北京市海淀区西土城路 25 号

邮寄地址　　北京 100088 信箱 8034 分箱　　邮编 100088

网　　　址　　http://www.cuplpress.com (网络实名：中国政法大学出版社)

电　　　话　　010-58908285(总编室) 58908433 （编辑部） 58908334(邮购部)

承　　　印　　三河市文阁印刷有限公司

开　　　本　　787mm×1092mm　1/16

印　　　张　　10

字　　　数　　235 千字

版　　　次　　2024 年 8 月第 1 版

印　　　次　　2024 年 8 月第 1 次印刷

定　　　价　　49.80 元

< 前言 >

各位 MTI 的准研究生们，谈到翻译，你们是不是也遇到了以下问题？

拿到原文，根本不知道从哪下手开始翻，开局即卡？

只会生搬硬套，句式单一，译文死板僵硬、不地道？

理解偏颇或有误，导致翻译不准或不对，失分严重？

那么，汉英翻译和英汉翻译相比，谁更难呢？

根据笔者多年翻译教学经验以及学生翻译学习情况反馈，汉英翻译是考生 MTI 考试的最大拦路虎。

为帮助考生解决这一难题，才有了《翻译硕士（MTI）汉英翻译技巧 12 讲》。这本书从考生的痛难点出发，聚焦汉英翻译，从"词—句—篇"3 大层面，由易到难，系统、详尽、精讲汉英翻译要点和翻译技巧，帮助考生解决"无从下手、翻译不准、翻译不好、失分严重"的问题。

《翻译硕士（MTI）汉英翻译技巧 12 讲》以"书课结合"的形式多元助力考生备考。

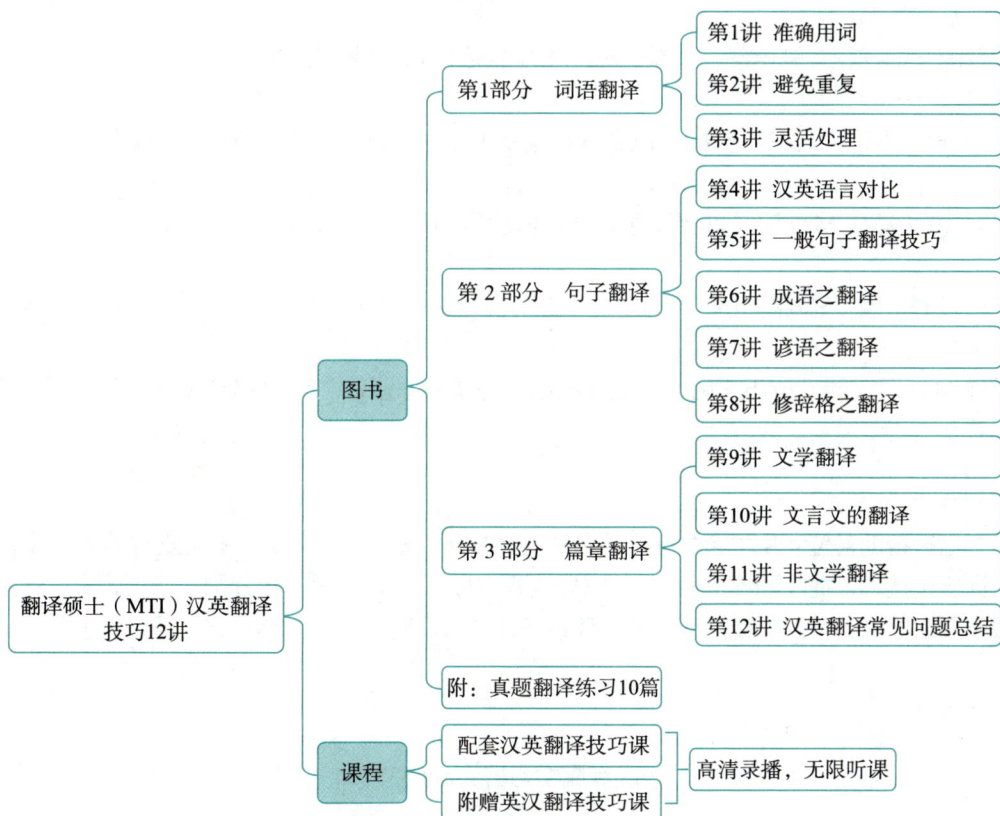

全书内容框架图：

- 翻译硕士（MTI）汉英翻译技巧12讲
  - 图书
    - 第1部分　词语翻译
      - 第1讲　准确用词
      - 第2讲　避免重复
      - 第3讲　灵活处理
    - 第2部分　句子翻译
      - 第4讲　汉英语言对比
      - 第5讲　一般句子翻译技巧
      - 第6讲　成语之翻译
      - 第7讲　谚语之翻译
      - 第8讲　修辞格之翻译
    - 第3部分　篇章翻译
      - 第9讲　文学翻译
      - 第10讲　文言文的翻译
      - 第11讲　非文学翻译
      - 第12讲　汉英翻译常见问题总结
    - 附：真题翻译练习10篇
  - 课程
    - 配套汉英翻译技巧课
    - 附赠英汉翻译技巧课 —— 高清录播，无限听课

全书内容框架图

内容设计

本书内容按照"词一句一篇"的顺序讲解翻译技巧，从源头开始解决翻译问题，由小到大，从具体到宏观，系统而又具有层次性，梯度式讲解汉英翻译，符合学生的学习习惯，知识体系较为科学。

书中译例大多选自经典名著、官方文件或部分高校的历年翻硕真题，具有代表性和权威性。所选译例多呈现 2 种版本的译文，可供学生对比分析，让学生明白好的译文好在哪里，不好的译文不好在哪里，以凸显翻译技巧的作用。此外，译例本着"汉英语言特点 / 区别→汉语原文→运用什么翻译技巧→运用翻译技巧后的译文优势在哪里"的逻辑框架进行分析，深入且细致，极具条理性和说服力。

全书共分 12 讲，每讲都设有【真题译 · 注 · 评】栏目，以部分高校的历年翻硕真题作为素材，对其中重要的翻译知识点进行注解和点评，并适当作一些拓展，更全面地助力考生备考。

书后附"真题翻译练习 10 篇"，供考生学后练技巧，使考生在理论学习的基础上通过做题实践应用所学翻译技巧，做到"学讲练结合、知行合一"。同时，考生可通过练习真题，提前了解真题难度和不同院校的汉英篇章翻译的考试风格，使其备考更有针对性。

最后，希望本书能够帮助广大考生在学习汉英翻译时少走一些弯路，使考生能够在较短时间内快速掌握实用汉英翻译技巧、提升汉英翻译能力、提高翻译得分率。

使用指南

Step 1　预习
建议同学们在正式开始学习之前先预习书中相应内容，熟悉所讲知识。

Step 2　听课
学习配套"汉英翻译技巧课"，以更好地理解书中所讲翻译技巧，增强学习效果。

Step 3　应用
练习 10 大高校 MTI 汉英翻译真题，通过做题应用所学技巧，输出学习成果。

Step 4　复盘
练后及时复盘，总结学习的薄弱之处，针对性地进行"再学习"，有的放矢，高效复习。

Step 5　拓展
掌握 MTI 汉英翻译技巧之后，考生可拓展学习本书附赠的"英汉翻译技巧课"，实现"汉英、英汉"齐头并进。

致读者——

该书旨在帮助各位考生学会灵活运用各种翻译技巧，提升译文质量，在短时间内有效掌握 MTI 汉英翻译应试技巧，提高翻译得分率。本书在编纂时，虽力求完美，但受限于各种因素，难免会有不足或不妥之处。若有纰漏或错误之处，还请各位读者及同仁志士能够及时反馈，给予指正。

12 讲专属学习群：806433254

罗老师小红书：2846713337（定期分享翻硕备考资料）

罗国强

< 目录 >

第 1 部分　词语翻译

第 2 部分　句子翻译

词语翻译

第 1 讲　准确用词

第 1 节　感情色彩

感情色彩是翻译准确用词的一个重要考量因素。词汇按照感情色彩可分为褒义词、贬义词和中性词。在翻译中，最好做到感情色彩一致——褒义词翻译成褒义词，贬义词翻译成贬义词，中性词也应翻译成中性词。但有时候原文褒义词在目的语中找不到对应的褒义词，可以退而求其次用中性词，但不能用贬义词；同样的，原文的贬义词在目的语中找不到对应的贬义词，也可以退而求其次用中性词，但不能用褒义词。

很多近义词感情色彩不同，如：

汉语词汇	英语词汇 + 感情色彩	
著名	famous （褒）	notorious （贬）
政治家	statesman （褒）	politician （贬）
结果	result （中性）	consequence （贬）
影响	influence （中性）	affect （贬）

译例 1　有名的

她父亲是一位有名的外科医生。

译文　Her father is a famous （褒） surgeon.

黄金荣是旧上海有名的大流氓。

译文　Huang Jinrong was a notorious （贬） rogue in Shanghai in the old times.

译例 2　由于

由于党的农业政策，我国千千万万农民走上了致富的道路。

译文　Thanks to （褒） the policies of the Communist Party of China on agriculture, millions of farmers in China are on the way of getting rich.

由于两次世界大战的爆发，各国人民蒙受了极大的灾难。

译文　People of all countries have suffered great calamities in consequence of （贬） the two world wars.

译例 3　想象力丰富

诗人应该具有丰富的想象力。

译文　A poet should have rich imagination （褒） .

真遗憾，你的想象力太丰富了。

译文　What a pity! You've got into wild flights of fancy. （贬）（flights of fancy：异想天开）

分析　相同的表达在不同句子中感情色彩也许不同。以上译例中，根据原句感情色彩，译文用词做到了感情色彩的一致，忠实地传达了原文的意义。

　　有时候原文中一些表面褒义或贬义的表达，根据语境判断，可能表达相反的感情色彩。所以感情色彩不能只看字面，还要看语境。如：

译例 4　可是青年人热烈的求知欲望和好高骛远的劲头，管它懂不懂，她还是如饥如渴地读下去。（杨沫《青春之歌》）

译文　Yet her youthful craving for knowledge, her aspiring spirit, made her read on eagerly whether she understood or not.

译例 5　其四，部队的指挥要给以独断专行的权力，要使其能独立作战，分区活动，不怕留在敌人背后，不怕被敌人切断。《周恩来选集》

译文　Fourth, commanders of the army units must be given the power to make independent decisions, so that they can operate independently in separate areas and have no fear of remaining behind enemy lines or of being cut off.

分析　"好高骛远"本为贬义，但在译例 4 中明显是褒义，理解为追求高远的精神；"独断专行"字面为贬义，但在译例 5 中理解为独立做出决定。两个译文均根据具体语境判断了原文用词的感情色彩，以褒义色彩呈现，做到了感情色彩与原文一致。

第 2 节　搭配习惯

　　搭配错误是汉英翻译中的常见错误。英语是讲究搭配的语言，搭配和单词用法有关，也和习惯用法有关。例如，Merry Christmas 和 Happy New Year，就不能说成 Happy Christmas 和 Merry New Year。汉英翻译时，译者要注意英语的搭配习惯。如：

汉语	错误表达	正确表达
学习知识	study knowledge	acquire knowledge
推动经济发展	promote economy	boost economy
实现梦想	achieve dreams	realize dreams
大雨	big rain	heavy rain
改善收入	improve income	increase income

译例 1　只有通过这些方式，人们才能在生活中取得进步，获得成功。

译文　Only in these ways can people achieve progress and success in their life.

译例 2　很明显，就是因为对未来缺乏自信才使得他们无法获得他们想要得到的成就。

译文　Obviously, it is the shortage of confidence for their future that makes it impossible for them to get attainments they want.

译例 3　中国位居世界前列。

译文　China ranks high on the world's league table.

分析　以上三个译例中画线部分均为错误搭配。译例 1 中，"取得进步"常用 make progress，而非 achieve progress；译例 2 中，"获得成就"可以译为 make achievements，get attainments 是错误搭配；译例 3 中，on the world's league table 也是错误搭配，通常"位居世界前列"的英语说法是 rank high in the world 或 at the top of the world。

　　所以，表达切莫胡编乱造，不要用一些没有把握的表达。平时阅读中注意单词的用法和搭配习惯，并尽可能用常用的、熟悉的表达和搭配。当不确定一个词的搭配是否恰当时，建议通过查阅英英词典或利用网络工具加以验证，切勿仅凭主观臆断。

第 3 节　语域区分

根据语言使用的场合，语言表达在正式程度上存在区别。比如，法律文件、科技文本中的语言较为正式，而口头交谈则偏口语化。在翻译中，单词也存在正式程度的差异，不同的单词适用于不同的文体。正式词用在正式文体中，非正式词则用在非正式文体中。学习单词的时候，尤其要注意那些非正式或正式的表达方式。正规词典中，非正式的单词一般会标注 infml.（informal 的缩写）或 collo.（colloquial 的缩写），正式单词会标注 fml.（formal 的缩写）。标记为非正式的单词要避免用在正式的文体中；同样，标记为正式的单词要避免用在口语化的文体中。对于那些无任何标记的单词，一般属于共核词（普通词），各种文体均可使用。

语域的选择绝非易事。总的原则是：原文是口语化的东西，译文也要口语化，避免使用学究式语言；原文是正式文本，译文也要相对正式，避免使用过于口语化的语言。

译例　我幼年读过书，虽然不多，可是足够读七侠五义与三国志演义什么的。我记得好几段聊斋，到如今还能说得很齐全动听，不但听的人都夸奖我的记性好，连我自己也觉得应该高兴。可是，我并念不懂聊斋的原文，那太深了；我所记得的几段，都是由小报上的"评讲聊斋"念来的——把原文变成白话，又添上些逗眼打趣，实在有个意思！（老舍《我这一辈子》）

译文　① I had some schooling when I was young. Though it wasn't much, it is was enough education for me to read such novels as *The Seven Heroes and Five Gallants* and *Three Kingdoms*. I know quite a few stories from *Strange Tales from Make-Do Studio* too, and I can retell them vividly even now. People admired me for such a wonderful memory, and I also felt proud of that gift. But I wasn't able to read the books in the original, because classical language was too abstruse. The stories I learned were from the literature columns in newspapers. They were rewritten in plain language and spiced with humour. Those stories were fascinating.

② I studied a bit when I was a boy. Not much, mind you, but enough to read *The Seven Knights and Five Heroes* and *Three Kingdoms* and things like that. I know quite a lot of stories in *Liao Zhai*, by heart—I could tell you them with all the details if you liked. They make good listening. Not that I can read the originals—that classical language is too hard for me. The bits I know I learned from those "Liao Zhai Stories Retold" columns in the papers. They are terrific. They turn the classical stuff into ordinary Chinese, and put jokes in too.（W. J. F. Jenner 译）

分析　两个译文都非常准确地传达了原文的意思，但从风格角度来看，译文②更胜一筹。汉语原文明显是口语体，就好像作者在和读者对话一样。译文②中画横线处都是偏口语的表达方式，有助于表现原文口语化的风格。口语化另外一个特征是"负重词"（heavy duty words）的使用。所谓"负重词"，是指像 take、make、put 这类简单但很常用的单词，它们的文体色彩都偏口语化。总而言之，两个译文在内容上都忠实于原文，但译文②语域色彩更加贴近原文。

想要在不同文体中做到恰当用词需要一个长期的过程。首先，要勤查词典，了解单词的正式程度；其次，要大量阅读不同文体的材料，培养好的语感。

真题译·注·评

◆◆◆ **译文对照** ◆◆◆

[1]翻开中国近现代画史，一位富于传奇色彩的女画家就会跃入眼帘，她就是我国著名画家潘玉良。一九四一年，[2]为参加法国巴黎春季沙龙展览会，潘玉良创作了油画作品《女人体》。在潘玉良的作品中，类似这样的题材有很多，但这幅作品的背后却有着一段不同寻常的故事。（安徽大学·真题）

Pan Yuliang is a famous and legendary paintress in the history of modern Chinese painting. In 1941, she created a painting *Woman Body* for the Spring Salon Exhibition held in Paris. Of her works, many are similar to the painting in terms of subjects. However, there is an unusual story behind the painting.

[3]2005 年安徽省博物馆在对潘玉良作品的修复保护中，意外发现该幅作品的画布上有被割伤修补的痕迹，作品的背面还有一段文字，[4]记录了作品被损修复的原因，"此画出品一九四一年巴黎春季沙龙[5]有德军人要求减价让与未允在画展闭幕先二日（一九四一年五月卅一日）发觉此画被割同时尚有当代名画家 VAK Dongen 大幅佳作亦被观者私地裁破也"。这一意外发现，为我们打开了一段尘封的历史，也为潘玉良研究增添了新的重要史料。

In 2005, Anhui Provincial Museum happened to find marks of cut and repairs when they were restoring and preserving her works. On the back of the painting it was written: This painting was drawn in 1941 for the Spring Salon Exhibition in Paris. One Germany officer wanted to get it at a discount, but it was refused. Two days before the end of the exhibition (May 31st, 1941), it was found to have been cut.

---

1 翻开中国近现代画史，一位富于传奇色彩的女画家就会跃入眼帘，她就是我国著名画家潘玉良。汉语可以简化为：在中国近现代画史中，有一位富于传奇色彩的女画家，她就是我国著名画家潘玉良。这样就避开了"翻开""跃入眼帘"这样的表达。翻译可以在意义不变的前提下，化繁为简，用简单熟悉的表达方式，而不是硬贴字面翻译。

2 为参加法国巴黎春季沙龙展览会，潘玉良创作了油画作品《女人体》。潘玉良这个名字在汉语原文中不断重复，英语用代词指代即可，不用重复名字；为参加法国巴黎春季沙龙展览会，是后面创作作品的目的，可以用 for 引导目的状语，放后面，同时去掉"参加"，做到译文的简化；油画作品，"作品"属于范畴词，省去不翻；法国巴黎春季沙龙展览会，"法国"不用翻，因为大家都知道巴黎就在法国，大家都知道的可以不讲。巴黎春季沙龙展览会可以理解为"在巴黎举办的春季沙龙展览会"，巴黎可以作地点状语放在后面。

3 汉英翻译中，最好先确定句子结构，确定主语和谓语动词。本句可以用 Anhui Provincial Museum 作主语，happened to find 作复合谓语。"在对潘玉良作品的修复保护中"可以译为 when 引导的时间状语从句，放在后面。"意外发现该幅作品的画布上有被割伤修补的痕迹"中的"画布"属于不言而明的信息，因为油画被割伤肯定是它的画布被割伤，故省去不译。

4 "记录了作品被损修复的原因"可以放在后面翻。作品的背面还有一段文字，"此画出品……"直接衔接很顺畅。翻译根据表达需要可以对原文表达顺序进行一定的调整。

5 "有德军人"，这里没法确定是军官还是士兵，officer 或 soldier 都可接受。

Several works by a famous contemporary painter VAK Dongen were also cut by someone privately. This record can account for the damage and restoration of the painting. This unexpected discovery reveals a history and provides new important historical information for studying the famous paintress Pan Yuliang.

◆◆◆ 知识点评 ◆◆◆

（温馨小贴士：此栏目有时为丰富译例，会拓展一些真题之外的译例进行讲解，该类译例会标注 拓 这一标识。）

（1）信息重组或替换

　　汉英翻译时，有时直译原文会造成译文不流畅，或是不符合目的语叙事论理的习惯。这时，在不改变原文意思的前提下，可以摆脱原文束缚，灵活对原文信息进行重组或替换，以写出更流畅、地道的译文。

译例 1　**翻开中国近现代画史，一位富于传奇色彩的女画家就会跃入眼帘，她就是我国著名画家潘玉良。**

译文　Pan Yuliang is a famous and legendary paintress in the history of modern Chinese painting.

分析　我们可以把原文信息重组为"在中国近现代画史中，潘玉良是一位著名的、富于传奇色彩的女画家"。重组后，介词"在"替代了原文的动词"翻开"；"著名""富于传奇色彩的"改为并列前置定语；"潘玉良"作主语，把后两句合并成一个句子。汉语原文简化的同时，译文也会相应地得到简化。如果把原文直译为"If we open the history of modern Chinese painting, a legendary paintress will come into our view. She is Pan Yuliang, a famous artist in our country."，译文不够简洁精炼，表达效果要差一些。

译例 2　拓**中欧都主张国际关系民主化，在许多国际重大事务上有共同利益，双方关系具有越来越重要的全球影响。**

译文　Both China and European Union advocate more democracy in international relationships and share common interests in major international affairs. Their bilateral relationship is exerting increasing international influence.

分析　"……化"在汉英时政文本翻译中出现的频率很高，有些有直接对应的英语词汇（大多以 -ize、-ized、-ization 结尾）可以使用；但大多没有直接对应的词汇可供使用，这时就需要对其进行替换。"化"为一个动词化后缀，常接在名词或形容词之后。这类结构的动词为弱势动词，其名词性强于动词性，体现的更多是"静态"语言的特点。而汉英两种语言中，英语为"静态"语言，常用名词，少用动词。故翻译该例时，译文将原文动词"民主化"替换为名词"民主"，同时根据调整的词性变化，进行信息重组，将原文"主张国际关系民主化"重组为"主张在国际关系中有更多的民主"，因此可以译为 advocate more democracy in international relationships。

译例 3　拓**世界因互联网而更多彩，生活因互联网而更丰富。**

译文　The Internet has brought a more colorful world and a more diversified lifestyle.

分析　如果把原文直译为"Thanks to the Internet, the world has become more colorful and lifestyle has become more diversified."，译文较为机械化，语言表述较为呆板，结构较为零散。原

文中"互联网"出现了两次，且"世界更多彩"和"生活更丰富"都是"互联网"带来的改变，通过梳理原文逻辑关系，翻译时先将原文信息重组为"互联网带来更多彩的世界、更丰富的生活"，译为：The Internet has brought a more colorful world and a more diversified lifestyle。相比直译，后者由 The Internet 作主语，brought 作谓语，将"互联网"拟人化，语言更为生动，且信息重组后的译文一顺而下，更为流畅。

（2）前置定语后置处理

汉语前置定语较为普遍，且有时较长，而英语不喜欢前置定语太长，长定语一般后置。考虑到英语表达习惯，汉语中的定语有时不能直译，可以灵活采用后置或部分后置的方法处理。

译例 4 **中国近现代画史**

译文 ① modern Chinese painting history

② the history of modern Chinese painting

分析 原文中，"中国近现代画"修饰"史"。如果把原文直译为译文①：modern Chinese painting history，就会存在表达错误，因为"modern Chinese painting"作为一个整体不能直接修饰后面的名词。翻译时可以参考译文②，使用名词所有格，定语后置，这样结构既符合英语语法，修饰关系也清晰。

译例 5 **法国巴黎春季沙龙展览会**

译文 ① Paris Spring Salon Exhibition held in France

② the Spring Salon Exhibition held in Paris

分析 原文中，"展览会"作为修饰对象，"巴黎春季沙龙"作前置定语，"法国"作地点状语。如果把原文直译为译文①：Paris Spring Salon Exhibition in France，那么前置定语就会偏长，不是一个好的译文。这时，可以参考译文②，把"巴黎"作为定语，后置处理，用过去分词短语 held in Paris 来表达。汉语中，表示"地点"的前置定语，英译时根据表达需要，可以后置处理。

译例 6 ㉕铁路、民航体制改革取得新进展。

译文 ① Further progress has been made in the railway and civil aviation system reform.

② Further progress has been made in the reform of the railway and civil aviation systems.

分析 原文中，"铁路、民航体制"修饰"改革"。译文①严格按照原文结构直译，将定语前置，偏长。前置定语偏长会导致结构失衡，且不利于读者理解。译文②用 of 引导后置定语，修饰 reform，符合英语的表达习惯，译文可读性也更强。

第 2 讲　避免重复

汉语中存在大量重复表达，而英语则倾向避免意义或表达形式的重复，除非有修辞或其他目的。汉英翻译中，往往删去一些重复的、可有可无的或已经包含在上下文中、不言而明的表达，也往往避开同一表达的反复使用。逐字逐句的字面翻译往往画蛇添足，不符合英语的表达习惯。翻译追求的是意义上的对等，而不是字对字、句对句的对等。汉英翻译中，避免重复的常见方式有省译、照应和替代。省译主要用于避免意义的重复，而照应和替代则主要用于避免形式的重复。

第 1 节　省译

1.1　省译范畴词

在英语中，通常一个单词本身就可以表明其范畴，不必再用表示范畴的词。如 flexibility 本身就表示一种态度，不用说 flexible attitude；red 本身就表示一种颜色，不用说 red in color。

汉语中则存在大量范畴词，尤其在一些四字表达中。汉语中的范畴词大多没有实际含义，只是为了构成一种搭配，限定前面词语的性质或范围，直接翻译到英语中不增加任何实质内容。这样直译的译文不仅冗长，而且不地道，因此汉英翻译时可以省译范畴词。汉语范畴词分名词范畴词和动词范畴词。

1.1.1　省译名词范畴词

- 紧张局势 tension
- 越轨行为 irregularities
- 犯罪现象 crimes
- 摇摆的局面 uncertainties
- 准备工作 preparation
- 促进和平统一大业 promote peaceful reunification
- 经济领域的改革 economic reform
- 密切合作的关系 close cooperation

以上画横线处均为范畴词，可省去不译。如"经济领域的改革"，"经济"本身就是一个领域，直接译为 economic reform 即可，省译范畴词"领域（field）"。

译例 1　他是在我不知道的情况下拿走它的。

译文　He took it without my knowledge.

分析　"我不知道"就是一种情况，因此翻译时范畴词"情况"不用翻译。

译例 2　在工作中，大家都需要杜绝浪费现象。

译文　We need put an end to waste in our work.

分析　"浪费"就是一种现象，因此"现象"这一范畴词不用翻译。

1.1.2 省译动词范畴词

汉语常用范畴词概括具体词，并不限于名词；对动词短语也可以进行类似的概括。如果这一概括没有实质意义，一般不用翻译出来，只需翻译该动词短语。如：

译例 3 **我们的部队采取了缓慢前进的方法。**

译文 Our troops advanced slowly.

分析 "缓慢前进"就是采取的具体方法，"方法"属于动词范畴词，意思已经被包含在"缓慢前进"中，可以省去不译。同时，也需省译前面的搭配动词"采取"。由此可见，范畴词常与其搭配动词同时省略。

译例 4 **当时东北处于敌强我弱的局面。**

译文 At that time, the enemy was still stronger than the people's forces in northeast China.

分析 "敌强我弱"本身就是一种局面，所以原文可简化为"当时东北敌强我弱"，汉英翻译时，省译范畴词"局面"，并不影响意思表达。其实判断能否省译范畴词的一种简单方法就是看省译后的表达和原文意思是否一致。

译例 5 **1989 年全国税收大检查，出现了对一些私营企业惩罚过重的现象。**

译文 In the 1989 national tax check-up, private enterprises were handed too heavy penalties.

分析 "对一些私营企业惩罚过重"本身就是一种现象，因此"出现了……现象"可以省去不译，没有必要直译为：there were situations where private enterprises were handed too heavy penalties。

但是如果范畴词本身具有实质意义，或者其意思并未包含在动词短语中，就要翻译出来。如：

译例 6 **中国一贯遵守和平共处的方针。**

译文 China has always followed a policy of peaceful coexistence.

译例 7 **而坚持社会主义，实行按劳分配的原则，就不会产生贫富过大的差距。**

译文 But if we stick to socialism and apply the principle of work-based distribution of income, wealth disparity will not be too great.

分析 译例 6 中，对中国来说，遵守的是一个具体的方针，此"方针"具有实质意义，不能省译，因为"和平共处"本身不一定包含"方针"的意思，也可以将其理解为一个具体做法，而不是"方针"。同理，译例 7 中，"原则"具有实质意义，表明我国按这个原则行事。此外，"按劳分配"本身并不一定包含"原则"的意思，省译后意思会有损失，译文读者可能会不知道"按劳分配"在我国是既定原则。

1.2 省译形容词或副词

汉语中有些形容词或副词用作修饰的时候，只是用来强调、增强气势或保持工整，本身并没有实质意义。汉语习惯在动词和形容词前加副词，在名词前加形容词，实际上很多时候加与不加的意思没有多大区别。例如，"胜利完成"中的"完成"本身带有成功的意思，省译"胜利"，意思并没有受到影响。

译例 8　只有**充分**发展商品经济，才能把经济**真正**搞活，使各企业增加效率。

译文　The development of a commodity economy is the only way to invigorate our economy and prompt enterprises to raise their efficiency.

分析　本句中，"充分""真正"只是为了加强语气，没有实质内容，可省去不译，意思不受影响。副词的翻译要具体问题具体分析。如果去掉副词没有造成意义的损失，可以省译，但如果副词具有区别性特征，一旦省译，会造成原文意义受损，翻译时就应该保留。例如 "run quickly" 中的 run 需要借助另一个词 quickly 来呈现 run 的程度，那么此处的 quickly 就有实质意义，不能省译。

译例 9　过去五年，从**外国进口**的汽车总量在不断下降。

译文　The number of imported automobiles has declined over the past five years.

分析　"进口汽车"肯定来自外国，所以"外国进口的汽车"不用译为"foreign imported automobiles"，可省译"外国"，将其译为"imported automobiles"。

另外，英语中有些动词本身包含了汉语中"副词 + 动词"的意思，所以在翻译中，只要选取了合适的动词，往往可以省略副词。如：

译例 10　人群**渐渐地**安静了下来。

译文　The crowd came to silence.

译例 11　我的姐姐又因为我不爱整洁而向我**唠叨地**劝诫了。

译文　My sister has been preaching at me again about my lack of neatness.

译例 12　中国政府**郑重**声明……

译文　The Chinese government declared...

分析　译例 10、11 中的副词"渐渐地""唠叨地"已经包含在动词 came to 和 preach 中，不必赘述。译例 12 中，原文中的"声明"意为"公开表态或说明真相"，是中性词，需借助"郑重"来强调中国政府声明的态度，但英语中的 declare（声明）一词意为 state officially and formally（正式说明），已经包含了 seriously（严肃、认真）的意味，故汉英翻译时可省译表示情感色彩的副词"郑重"一词。

以上译例告诉我们，汉英翻译中选择合适的动词很重要，若动词选取合适，译文不仅能精准传达原文意思，而且表达更为简洁、地道。

1.3　省译动词

汉语中，动名词结构非常普遍。有时候，动词意思在句中可有可无，只构成一种搭配，省译之后译文意思不但不受影响，结构也会更为简洁，语言更为精炼。很多动词在句中并没有实质意义，翻译时应注意辨别。

译例 13　新中国的成立，标志着中华民族**实现了**空前的大团结。

译文　The foundation of the People's Republic of China in 1949 marked an unprecedented great unity of the Chinese nation.

分析　"标志着中华民族实现了空前的大团结"和"标志着中华民族空前的大团结"没有任何区别，所以可省译动词"实现"。汉语多用"动词＋名词"结构，英语多用名词短语。很多时候，汉英翻译可以省译汉语的动词，将汉语的"动词＋名词"结构译为名词短语，这样译文更简洁、地道。

译例14　维护世界和平，促进共同发展，谋求合作共赢，是各国人民的共同愿望，也是不可抗拒的当今时代潮流。中国高举和平、发展、合作的旗帜，坚持走和平发展道路，与世界各国一道，共同致力于建设一个持久和平、共同发展的和谐世界。

译文　Universal peace, common development and win-win cooperation are the common wish of people all over the world and also an irreversible trend of our times. In this context, China, in a spirit of peace, development and cooperation, follows the path of peaceful development and works with other countries for a harmonious world of everlasting peace and common prosperity.

分析　汉语动词的使用多于英语，英语多用名词短语，避免动词重复堆砌。本例中，将"维护世界和平，促进共同发展，谋求合作共赢"三个动词短语译为三个名词短语，不仅简洁，而且符合英语的表达习惯。但并不是说，所有汉语动名词结构都能去掉动词，要看去掉之后原文意思是否有损。

1.4　同义表达

1.4.1　四字结构

汉语表达讲究平衡、追求对称，尤其是四字词组，用两个同义词或近义词组成工整对仗的对称结构。例如，贪官污吏，"贪官"和"污吏"内涵相同，翻译一半即可。再看一些例子：

- 生动活泼 lively
- 浓妆艳抹 heavily made up
- 深仇大恨 deep hatred
- 街谈巷议 street gossip
- 土崩瓦解 fall apart
- 光辉灿烂 brilliant
- 打击报复 retaliate
- 医德医风 medical ethics

以上几个四字词组中，每个词组的前后两项表示的是同一个意思，在翻译时，只要译出其中一项即可，不必字字对译。但是，并不是说所有四字表达都存在意义重复，需具体问题具体分析。例如，"鸟语花香"就包含两个意思，并不存在重复，两项含义均需译出。

1.4.2　并列成分

汉语中行文常常用两个并列的词语或词组，甚至用两个并列的句子来表示强调或加强语气，通过这种手段以达到对仗工整、渲染气氛的效果。很多时候，这些并列成分表达角度不同，但内涵相同，我们可以翻译其中一个或概括其内涵，而不必重复表达相同的意思。如：

- 神不知，鬼不觉 stealthily
- 取之不尽，用之不竭 inexhaustible
- 攻无不克，战无不胜 invincible
- 主持公道，伸张正义 uphold justice

译例15　在长期的革命历程中，各民主党派和中国共产党同呼吸共命运。

译文　In the protracted process of the Chinese revolution, the various democratic parties shared a common fate with the Communist Party of China.

分析　"同呼吸"与"共命运"内涵相同，如果译为 breathed together and shared a common fate，译文不仅啰唆，而且行文呆板，令人费解。

译例16　那件令人不快的事件，已经搞得满城风雨、人人皆知了。

译文　There has been much publicity about the unpleasant case.

分析　"满城风雨""人人皆知"意义重叠，只需要把其整体意义概括出来即可。

译例17　我国人民在中国共产党第十五次全国代表大会的精神鼓舞下，正沿着建设有中国特色的社会主义道路，满怀信心、昂首阔步地迈向 21 世纪。

译文　Inspired by the spirit of the 15th National Congress of the Communist Party of China, the people of China are advancing confidently towards the 21st century along the road to socialism with Chinese characteristics.

分析　本句中，"满怀信心""昂首阔步"这两个词语内涵相同，它们合在一起其实表达的就是"自信"的意思，翻译时只需把"满怀信心"这一意义表达出来即可。

1.4.3　双动词结构

汉语中存在大量的双动词现象，即两个动词并列使用，如"调整和优化""提高和加强""加强和完善"，主要是为了加强语气。很多双动词表达中，一个动词的意思往往已经包含了另一个动词的意思，只需翻一个即可。但是并不是每一组双动词一定有语义重复，要看意思是否有重叠。

译例18　我认为关键是进一步解放思想，进一步解放和发展社会生产力，进一步解放和增强社会活力，打破一切体制机制的障碍。

译文　The key, I believe, is to further free our mind, unshackle productivity, unleash social dynamism and break all institutional obstacles to development.

分析　解放生产力一定会导致生产力的发展，所以"发展"不用另外强调；同样地，解放社会活力也一定会导致社会活力增强，"增强"也不用翻。双动词结构中，如果一个动词意义属于不言而明的信息，翻译中可以省去不译。

译例19　为了巩固经济社会发展良好势头，我们将继续加强和改善宏观调控。

译文　We will continue to improve macro-control to maintain the good momentum of socioeconomic development.

分析　本句中，"加强"与"改善"意思相近，翻译一个即可，否则译文会显得啰唆。

1.5 语境包含的意思

有些意思已经暗含在上下文语境中，可以省去不译，并不影响读者对译文的理解。汉英翻译和英汉翻译均存在这种现象。翻译首先要理解透原文，而不是不加分析，逐字逐句地翻译。

译例20 他们从地上爬起来，揩干净身上的血迹，掩埋好同伴的尸首，他们又继续战斗了。

译文 They picked themselves up, wiped off the blood, buried their fallen comrades and went into battle again.

分析 画横线处均不需要翻译，因为意思已经包含在语境中。爬肯定是"从地上"爬起来，揩干净血迹，肯定是揩干净"身上的"血迹，掩埋同伴就是掩埋同伴"尸首"的意思。画横线处都是不言而明的信息，英译时不用另外强调。

译例21 前进袜厂几十年如一日地生产一种"前进"牌线袜，这种袜子穿在脚上透气性能还好，可是你一开始走路它就开始前进，它随着你的步伐，慢慢从脚腕儿退至脚后跟，再退至脚心最终堆积至脚尖。（重庆大学·真题）

译文 The factory has been producing Advance-brand socks for several decades. The socks are fairly breathable, but when you walk, they slip slowly from your ankle to heel with your step and then to the middle of your feet and ultimately to your tiptoe.

分析 "袜子透气"肯定是穿在脚上透气，这是不言而明的信息，省译"穿在脚上"不会影响译文理解，如果翻译出来，反而显得多余。另外，"透气性能"中的"性能"可以看作范畴词，略去不译。由此可见，汉英翻译中，有时在意义不变的前提下，可以一定程度上简化汉语进行省译，从而使译文表达更加简单。

第 2 节　照应

照应是"语篇中的指代成分与指称或所指对象之间的相互解释关系"，是语篇实现结构衔接和语义连贯的一种重要手段，同时也是避免原词重复的重要手段。英语中的照应关系分为人称照应、指示照应和比较照应。本节将重点分析人称照应和指示照应在汉英翻译中的运用。

2.1　人称照应

人称照应是指用代词指代上下文出现的对象，具备这一功能的有人称代词和物主代词。使用人称照应可以避免重复表达，同时有助于译文的简洁、精炼和地道。

译例 1 中国作为后发现代化国家，极其需要借鉴国际经验。同时，在和平崛起进程中，中国又要以自己为主，来关注和解决自己的问题。这就是说，中国的现代化一定要有中国特色。

译文 ① As a late-starter committed to modernization, China is in dire need of drawing international experience. Meanwhile, it has to focus on and address problems mainly by itself in a peaceful rise, which means its modernization must bear its own characteristics.

② As a new comer striving for modernization, China is badly in need of drawing experience from international practice. At the same time, China must rely on itself to address and resolve problems arising in the process of her peaceful rise. In other words, China's modernization must bear its own unique characteristics.

分析 原词重复在汉语中是普遍现象，而避免原词重复是英语句子的一大特点。原文中"中国"出现了四次，在英译时应尽量避免原词重复。译文①在第一次使用"China"之后，分别用物主代词 it 和 its 指代，不仅语义关系清楚，也更简洁和地道。译文②基本直译原文，"China"连续重复三次，不符合英语避免重复的表达习惯。故译文①更好一些。

译例 2 翻开中国近现代画史，一位富于传奇色彩的女画家就会跃入眼帘，她就是我国著名画家潘玉良。一九四一年，为参加法国巴黎春季沙龙展览会，潘玉良创作了油画作品《女人体》。在潘玉良的作品中，类似这样的题材有很多，但这幅作品的背后却有着一段不同寻常的故事。（安徽大学·真题）

译文 ① Pan Yuliang is a famous and legendary paintress in the history of modern Chinese painting. In 1941, she created a painting *Woman Body* for the Spring Salon Exhibition held in Paris. Of her works, many are similar to the painting in terms of subjects. However, there is an unusual story behind the painting.

② When we recall the history of modern Chinese painting, a legendary female painter will come into our view. She is Pan Yuliang, a famous painter in China. In 1941, Pan Yuliang created an oil painting *Woman's Body* for the spring salon exhibition in Paris. Though there are many works with the same theme in Pan's works, *Woman's Body* has a unique story behind it.

分析 原文"潘玉良"这个名字出现三次，译文①第二次和第三次分别用人称单词 she 和 her 指代，构成人称照应，意义连贯、衔接合理。译文②出现了原名重复以及姓氏 Pan，用词单调、重复，不符合英语的用词特点，译文也生硬、不地道。故译文①更好一些。

2.2 指示照应

指示照应是用定冠词（the）、指示代词（this/these/that/those）、时间或地点副词（now/then/here/there）来表示照应关系，通过事物在时间或空间上的远近来确定所指对象。指示照应也是避免重复、实现译文简洁精炼的重要手段。

译例 3 中国特色社会主义进入新时代，我国社会主要矛盾已经转化为人民日益增长的美好生活需要和不平衡不充分的发展之间的矛盾。必须认识到，我国社会主要矛盾的变化是关系全局的历史性变化，对党和国家工作提出了许多新要求。

必须认识到，我国社会主要矛盾的变化，没有改变我们对我国社会主义所处历史阶段的判断，我国仍处于并将长期处于社会主义初级阶段的基本国情没有变，我国是世界最大发展中国家的国际地位没有变。（扬州大学·真题）

译文 As China has entered a new era of building socialism with Chinese characteristics, the major social contradiction has shifted to one between the ever-growing need for a better life and unbalanced and inadequate development. We must realize that the evolution is a historic change concerning the overall situation, bringing many new requirements for the work of both the Party and the country.

We must also realize the evolution doesn't change our judgement of the historical stage where China's socialism stands. The basic reality hasn't been changed that China is still in the primary stage of socialism and will last for a long time, which remains the largest developing country in the world.

分析 原文中"我国社会主要矛盾的变化"就指前面"我国社会主要矛盾已经转化为人民日益增长的美好生活需要和不平衡不充分的发展之间的矛盾"这一变化，所以翻译时用定冠词加"变化"指示照应即可，定冠词 the 可以指代前面提到的信息，为避免重复，使用"evolution"表示变化，"the evolution"言简意赅地传达了原文的意思。如果直译为 the change in the major social contradiction，译文将变得冗长、啰嗦。

译例 4 只有通过技术创新，大力发展新产品制备技术和深加工技术，延伸产业链，拓宽产品幅度，实现产品的高性能化、专用化、绿色化和高附加值化，才能优化产品的结构，提高产业的竞争力和为国民经济相关产业的配套能力。（北京林业大学·真题）

译文 We should innovate technologically, developing advanced manufacturing and processing technologies for new products; we should extend the industrial chain and diversify products; and we should make high-performance products and make specialized, green and high value-added products. Only by doing these things can we optimize product mix, increase industrial competitiveness and improve the supporting capacity for other relevant industries in our country.

分析　原文"只有通过……高附加值化"属于方式状语。如果直译该状语，无论放句首还是句尾，译文都将变得冗长、结构臃肿，因此可以分译，先将方式状语单独译成一个完整的句子"We should innovate technologically...high value-added products."，再用"Only by doing these things"进行语义衔接。其中，these things 指代前面提到的一系列做法，断句后 these 作指示照应，使译文变得语义关系清楚、逻辑清晰、衔接顺畅。

第 3 节　替代

汉语往往重复相同的表达方式，但英语不喜欢重复（修辞等特殊原因除外），英语喜欢用不同的表达方式表达相同的意思，以使表达多样化。了解英语的这一特点有助于译文更为地道。

译例 1　世界正在经历最大的、史无前例的合并与收购浪潮。这次浪潮以前所未有的力量从美国扩展到欧洲，再到新兴国家。在这些国家，许多人正目睹这一过程，担心这一商业集中的浪潮是否会转变为一个无法控制的反竞争力量。

毫无疑问大公司越来越大，越来越强。1982 年，跨国公司在国际贸易中占据的份额不到20%。今天，这个数据已经超过 25%，并且还在快速增长中。在对外开放并且欢迎外国投资的经济体中，跨国公司在生产中占的比例越来越大。举个例子，阿根廷，在 20 世纪 90 年代初的改革后，在 200 家最大公司的工业产量中跨国公司占的比例从 43% 增加到将近 70%。

译文　The world is going through the biggest wave of mergers and acquisitions ever witnessed. The process sweeps from America to Europe and reaches the emerging countries with unsurpassed might. Many in these countries are looking at this process and worrying whether the wave of business concentration will turn into an uncontrollable anti-competitive force.

There's no question that the big are getting bigger and more powerful. Multinational corporations accounted for less than 20% of international trade in 1982. Today the figure is more than 25% and growing rapidly. International affiliates account for a fast-growing segment of production in economies that open up and welcome foreign investment. In Argentina, for instance, after the reforms of the early 1990s, multinationals went from 43% to almost 70% of the industrial production of the 200 largest firms.

分析　第一段中，"合并与收购"和"商业集中"内涵相同，只不过"商业集中"为"合并与收购"的替代表达。在翻译时，译文为了避免原词重复，也采取了替代的翻译方法，将两处分别译为 mergers and acquisitions 和 business concentration。在第二段中，"跨国公司"出现了三次，为避免重复，翻译时分别用 Multinational corporations、International affiliates 和 multinationals 指代。其中，International affiliates 字面意思为跨国公司在各地的分支机构，但在本句语境中，其实指的就是跨国公司。

译例 2　如果吉米·赫法今天还活着，他很可能代表公务员这个群体。1960 年，当赫法的Teamsters 工会处于黄金期时，十个美国公务员中只有一个参加工会。现在，这一比例为 36%。2009 年，美国公有制部门工会成员的数量超过了私有制部门工会成员的数量。在英国，一半以上的公有制部门工人参加工会，但在私有制部门，这一比例只有大约15%。

译文 If Jimmy Hoffa were alive today, he would probably represent civil servants. When Hoffa's Teamsters was in its prime in 1960, only one in ten American government workers belonged to a union; now 36% do. In 2009 the number of unionists in America's public sector passed that of their fellow members in the private sector. In Britain, more than half of public-sector workers but only about 15% of private-sector ones are unionized.

分析 本例中有两处涉及重复，一处为"公务员"，一处为"参加工会"。为避免重复，翻译时用 government workers 替代 civil servants（二者都表示"公务员"的意思）；用 are unionized 替代 belonged to a union（二者都表示"参加工会"的意思）。

译例 3 过去十年，所谓的商业方法获得了几千个专利。Amazon. com 因为"一键式"在线支付系统获得一个专利。Merrill Lynch 因为资产分配方法获得专利。某发明家因为发明了举起盒子的技术也获得专利。

译文 Over the past decade, thousands of patents have been granted for what are called business methods. Amazon. com received one for its "one-click" online payment system. Merrill Lynch got legal protection for an asset allocation strategy. One inventor patented a technique for lifting a box.

分析 本例中，原文"获得专利"出现了四次。在翻译时，为避免重复，后三次分别译为 received one（one 作代词，指代 a patent）、got legal protection 和 patented。got legal protection 就是"获得专利"的意思，因为专利本质上就是一种法律保护，所以避免表达重复，除了换一个近义的表达方式，还可以换个角度进行解释。patent 作动词，意为"获得专利权"，在文中名词动用，因此汉英翻译时词性转变也是避免重复的重要方式。

在汉英翻译中，用丰富多彩而又贴切得当的语言形式，把反复出现而又意思不变的词语译得生动活泼，这就是所谓翻译中的表达多样性。在汉语原文中，同样的一个词语往往会反复使用，如果把它们翻译得千篇一律，英语译文就会显得词语贫乏、枯燥无味。在不同的上下文中，对这些词语用不同的译文进行处理，而译出同样的语意，就能使整篇译文或整部译著词语丰富、生动活泼。

在《红楼梦》这部巨著中，同一个成语往往反复出现多次，甚至十几次。杨宪益和戴乃迭翻译的《红楼梦》就充分显示了翻译中的表达多样性。如：

译例 4　魂不附体

贾瑞听了，魂不附体。（第二十回）

译文 Jia Rui nearly gave up the ghost.

邢王二夫人等在里头也听见了，都唬得魂不附体，并无一言，只有啼哭。（第一百一十二回）

译文 Their Ladyships overhearing this inside were frightened out of their wits. Speechless, they could only sob.

译例 5　得陇望蜀

我说你"得陇望蜀"呢。（第四十八回）

译文 The more you get, the more you want!

得陇望蜀，人之常情。（第七十六回）

译文 It's only natural for a man to hanker for more.

只因薛蟠是天性"得陇望蜀"的，……（第八十回）

译文 Now Xue Pan was a living example of the saying "To covet the land of Shu after getting the region of Long" ...

译例 6 一败涂地

必须先从家里自杀自灭起来，才能一败涂地呢！（第七十四回）

译文 We must start killing each other first before our family can be completely destroyed.

往后子孙遇见不得意的事，还是点儿底子，不到一败涂地。（第九十二回）

译文 Then in future, if things go badly for our descendants, they'll have something to fall back on and won't be bankrupted.

完了，完了！不料我们一败涂地如此！（第一百零五回）

译文 We're done for, done for! To think that we should be reduced to this!

真题译·注·评

◆◆◆ **译文对照** ◆◆◆

　　改革开放30多年来，[1]西藏[2]通过深化改革和扩大开放积极推动全区商业、对外贸易和旅游产业加快发展，[3]不仅增强了与内地的交流，同时也加强了与世界的联系和合作。

　　Over the last 30 years since reform and opening up, Xizang, an autonomous region in southwestern China, has been committed to the development of commerce, foreign trade and tourism by deepening reform and opening up. This has strengthened its communication and cooperation with other parts of China and foreign countries as well.

　　1993 年，西藏与全国一道开始建立[4]"框架一致、体制衔接"的社会主义市场经济体制。目前，西藏已经深深融入全国统一的市场体系，来自全国和世界各地的商品源源不断地进入西藏，[5]丰富城乡市场，提高百姓生活质量。西藏的名、优、特产品及民族手工业产品，大量进入全国市场。

　　In 1993, Xizang began to develop the socialist market economy with the rest of the country, growing into a new system within the same framework. Now, Xizang has been fully integrated into the whole market system of China. Various commodities produced both at home and abroad have kept

---

　　1　西藏。西藏是中国西南部的一个自治区，对外翻译时最好补上这个背景。有些重要的社会文化背景我们都知道，但外国读者可能不知道，予以补上，能在准确翻译的基础上向世界传达中国社会文化知识。

　　2　"深化改革和扩大开放"可以理解为"深化改革开放"，故"深化"和"扩大"这一双动词结构只译"深化（deepen）"即可，省译"扩大"，后面加"改革"和"开放"两个宾语；"积极推动"中的"积极"可以省译，因为西藏政府去推动这个事情，肯定是积极的，而不是被迫或被动的，汉语中有些副词意义已经暗含在语境中，可以省译；"全区"指西藏自治区，可以省译，因为上下文已经很明显，这些事情发生在西藏，注意识别汉语多余的背景信息。"通过深化改革和扩大开放"可以译为 by 引导的方式状语，放在句尾。

　　3　不仅增强了与内地的交流，同时也加强了与世界的联系和合作。这句话在汉语中是无主句，英语需要补充一个主语。根据上下文可知，主语指的是前半句内容，翻译时可以用 This 指代前半句，作主语。

　　4　"框架一致、体制衔接"的社会主义市场经济体制。社会主义市场经济本身就是一种体制，"体制"属于范畴词，可以省译；"框架一致、体制衔接"可以理解为"同一框架内的新体制"，翻译时意义可以重组合并，使译文更加简洁、地道。

　　5　来自全国和世界各地的商品源源不断地进入西藏，产生的结果就是：丰富城乡市场，提高百姓生活质量。可以直接用分词引导结果状语，译为"enriching its urban and rural markets and improving people's life"。

flooding into the region, enriching its urban and rural markets and improving people's life. [6]Meanwhile, well-known and quality products with local characteristics and some ethnically styled handicrafts are sold all over the country.

西藏与世界的经济联系日益密切。2012 年，全区进出口总额为 34.24 亿美元，是 1953 年 0.04 亿美元的 850 多倍，年均增长 12.1%。

Xizang enjoys an increasingly close economic tie with the outside world. In 2012, its imports and exports totaled $3.424 billion, while in 1953 that was only $4 million. The total value has increased by over 850 times with an annual growth of 12.1% on average.

截至 2012 年底，西藏 [7]实际利用外资 4.7 亿美元。西藏立足区位优势，加强与印度、尼泊尔等周边国家的友好合作，[8]实施面向南亚的陆路贸易大通道建设，建设吉隆、樟木、亚东、普兰和日屋口岸，大力发展边境贸易。

By the end of 2012, Xizang had used foreign investment totaling $470 million. Exploiting its geographical conditions, it has enhanced friendly cooperation with neighboring partners, like India and Nepal. To facilitate border trade, it built an overland trade passage to South Asia, and built trading centers in such port cities as Gyirong, Zhangmu, Yatung, Pulan and Riwu.

◆◆◆ 知识点评 ◆◆◆

（1）汉语理解并非易事

译例 1 改革开放 30 多年来，西藏通过深化改革和扩大开放积极推动全区商业、对外贸易和旅游产业加快发展，不仅增强了与内地的交流，同时也加强了与世界的联系和合作。

译文 This has strengthened its communication and cooperation with other parts of China and foreign countries as well.

分析 如果直译画横线处，外国读者可能会理解为"与世界有联系和合作，但与内地只有交流，没有合作"，至少他们没法获得与内地有合作的信息。但事实上，与内地不可能只有交流没有合作。所以首先要进行逻辑推理，理解透原文，包括一些字里行间没有明确表达但暗含的意思。本句中，"交流"其实相当于"联系"，英语中用一个词 communication 即可，不需要既用 communication 又用 contact。根据以上分析，汉语可以重组为"不仅增强了与内地的交流与合作，同时也加强了与世界的交流和合作"。上述译文就是意义重组后的呈现。

6　外地产品进入西藏的同时，西藏本地产品肯定会销往外地。增译 Meanwhile 可以使译文更加通顺，译出原文汉语暗含之义。

7　实际利用。"实际"没有实质意义，属于多余的副词修饰，省译。

8　实施面向南亚的陆路贸易大通道建设，可以重组为"建设面向南亚的陆路贸易大通道"，省译"实施"，简化译文。

译例 2　拓 19 世纪中叶以后，由于列强的野蛮侵略和封建统治的无能，中华民族陷入了**丧权辱国**、**民不聊生**的悲惨境地。

译文　Since the 1850s, China had been reduced by foreign invasion and feudal incompetence to a dire situation where the sovereignty was violated, the nation was humiliated and people lived in extreme poverty.

分析　"丧权辱国"中的"丧权"，很多同学将其理解为丧失主权，直接翻译成 the sovereignty was lost，其实是误译。中国从来没有丧失过主权，哪怕在近代也是一个独立的国家，只是主权受到侵犯，并没有完全丧失，所以翻译成 the sovereignty was violated。汉语理解有时需要跳脱字面，考虑当时的背景。

（2）汉语表达的统一与英语用词的多元

以上这篇文章，"西藏"原词重复过很多次，但翻译成英语不能次次都原词对应，可以用各种方式避免重复：有时可以不翻，有时可以用代词指代，有时可以转化成其他的表达。但无论怎么指代、转化，都不能影响译文的理解，尤其不能有歧义。另外，根据表达的需要，有时重复原词也是必要的。

译例 3　来自全国和世界各地的商品源源不断地进入**西藏**，丰富城乡市场，提高百姓生活质量。**西藏**的名、优、特产品及民族手工业产品，大量进入全国市场。

译文　Various commodities produced both at home and abroad have kept flooding into the region, enriching its urban and rural markets and improving people's life. Meanwhile, well-known and quality products with local characteristics and some ethnically styled handicrafts are sold all over the country.

分析　以上两个西藏，一个指代翻译成 the region，一个转化翻译为 local，将译文表达多元化处理。

译例 4　截至 2012 年底，西藏实际利用外资 4.7 亿美元。**西藏**立足区位优势，加强与印度、尼泊尔等周边国家的友好合作……

译文　By the end of 2012, Xizang had used foreign investment totaling $470 million. Exploiting its geographical conditions, it has enhanced friendly cooperation with neighboring partners, like India and Nepal.

分析　代词指代是英语避免重复的有效方式。本例在英译第二个西藏时，采取了用代词 it 指代的方式，避免了原词重复。汉英翻译要学会多用代词指代重复出现的信息，但前提是指代不能有误，不能有歧义，不能影响读者理解。

第3讲 灵活处理

第1节 具体译法

由于汉英两种语言的差别，我们在翻译中经常使用具体译法，也就是具体化的翻译方法。所谓具体译法，就是在翻译过程中把原文中抽象或者是比较抽象的单词、词组、成语或句子用具体或者是比较具体的单词、词组、成语或句子来进行翻译，以消除或减少语言差异给翻译带来的损失，从而使译文产生与原文相同的效果，可读性更强。

具体译法的优势在于以生动具体的形象来表达原文中比较抽象的概念，使读者能够通过生动具体的形象来感受语言想要表达的意思。如：

汉语	英语
进退两难	between the devil and the deep blue sea
快活的人	a jolly dog
脾气暴躁的人	a surly dog
勤奋卖力的人	a work horse
最不受欢迎的东西	garlic for dessert
得到许可	get the green light
保密	keep sth. under one's hat
大吵大闹	raise the roof
公开认错	stand in a white sheet
话中有话	with the tongue in the cheek
获得全胜	sweep the board
机敏	keep one's eyes on the ball
坚决反对	set one's face against
侥幸	by the skin of one's teeth
结为良缘	win the hand of
截然不同	oil and vinegar
家丑	a skeleton in the cupboard
觉得可疑	smell a rat
鲁莽的人	a bull in a china shop
捏造	pull sth. out of one's hat

汉语	英语
告发	put the finger on
干苦差事	hold the baby
恻隐之心	the milk of human kindness
简言之	in a nutshell

以上例子中，英语相比汉语更加具体，如 between the devil and the deep blue sea，相比汉语的"进退两难"，在读者脑海中是一幅更加具体的画面。具体译法是翻译的一个选择，但不是唯一的选择。如"保密"可以译为更加具体的"keep sth. under one's hat"，也可以直译为"keep...a secret"。译文往往是多元化的，具体译法可以给译者提供另外一个翻译的角度，所以译者在平日阅读时可以留意并积累一些具体化的表达方式以丰富自己的翻译表达。内容具体的表达方式优点在于表达形象，这在文学作品翻译中经常可以看到，但在严肃的正式文体中要慎用，因为以上这些具体译法，在语域上，文体都不够正式。

译例 1　他每天要处理许多棘手的问题。

译文　He has many hot potatoes to handle every day.

译例 2　他新雇来的女佣人懒得出奇，饭量倒很大，真是一个无用而又累赘的东西。

译文　His newly employed woman servant was extremely lazy and ate a lot, no more than a white elephant.

译例 3　我不敢肯定我能赢得这个荣誉，这尚未定局。

译文　I'm not sure whether I can win the honor; it's a bird in the bush.

译例 4　这个男孩真粗心，他的书本都已经折角了。

译文　This boy is too careless, whose books all are dog-eared.

译例 5　你应该分清好坏。

译文　You should separate the sheep from the goats.

译例 6　我们决不能姑息坏人。

译文　We should never warm snakes in our bosoms.

译例 7　还有点美中不足的地方，早晨给车夫们摆饭的时节，祥子几乎和人打起来。

（老舍《骆驼祥子》，第十四章）

译文　Another fly in the ointment was that Xiangzi had nearly got into a fight that morning when the rickshaw pullers were having their feast.

译例 8　等他自作自受，少不得要自己败露的。（曹雪芹《红楼梦》，第八十一回）

译文　We'd better give her rope to hang herself—she's bound to give herself away one of these days.

分析　我们可以看出上面的译文都采用了具体化的翻译技巧，用日常生活中人们经常见到的东西、经常说的话语来表达，这样的译文不仅忠实于原文，也更加形象生动。

第 2 节　抽象译法

　　和具体译法相反，抽象译法指用抽象的或比较抽象的表达来翻译具体的或比较具体的表达。为了译文的忠实与通顺，我们有时需要把原文中带有具体意义或具体形象的单词、词组、成语或句子进行抽象化处理。

　　汉语中存在大量范畴词。范畴词对前面的名词性质进行解释，使表达更为具体，如在"同情"后面加"心理"，对读者来说，意义更为具体。前面的"1.1.1　省译名词范畴词"也是抽象译法的一种。一旦省译名词范畴词，译文便只剩一个抽象名词。如：

汉语	英语	汉语	英语
残暴行为	brutality	冷漠态度	indifference
同情心理	sympathy	蒸馏过程	distillation
同化作用	assimilation	解决方法	solution
发展过程	development	走私活动	smuggling
无知的表现	innocence	蛮干作风	fool-hardiness
谦虚态度	modesty	沮丧情绪	dejection
稳定性	stability	转化过程	transformation

译例 1　我们要重视沿海与内地的贫富差距问题。

译文　We must pay close attention to the wealth gap between coastal and inland areas.

分析　原文中，"差距问题"中的"问题"是范畴词，对"差距"性质进行解释。范畴词的使用使表达更为具体。但对英语来说，既然有"差距"，就肯定存在"问题"，不需要赘述。因此，翻译中对"差距问题"进行抽象化处理，译为 wealth gap，符合英语的表达习惯。

　　汉语中的成语或习语往往需要抽象处理，因为它们包含的具体形象或背后的故事很难直接移植到英语文化中。例如，"画蛇添足"是具体的故事，但翻译的时候不可能描述具体故事情节，而是把故事所呈现的道理用抽象的表达呈现出来。如：

汉语	英语
灯红酒绿	dissipated and luxurious
鸡毛蒜皮	trifling
开门见山	come straight to the point

续表

汉语	英语
狗急跳墙	a cornered beast will do something desperate
铜墙铁壁	an impregnable fortress
黔驴技穷	at one's wits' end
生龙活虎	bursting with energy
粗枝大叶	to be crude and careless
单枪匹马	to be single-handed in doing sth.

　　汉语成语绝大多数不能直译，不能保留原文具体的形象，否则译文没有可读性。如果把"粗枝大叶"译为 with big branches and large leaves，不仅没有忠实原文的意思，译文读者也会感到困惑。把原成语中具体的形象以抽象的表达翻译出来，至少译出了原文的意思。翻译成语时，当形式与意义发生冲突的时候，还是取意为上。

译例 2　真正的好朋友应该是雪中送炭。

译文　A real good friend should be one offering timely help.

译例 3　这是他们夫妻之间的事情，你去插一脚干吗？

译文　That's a business of their own, between husband and wife. Why should you get involved in it?

译例 4　他万万没想到在他前进的道路上竟会出现这么多拦路虎！

译文　He had never expected that so many obstacles would stand in his way.

译例 5　我不敢班门弄斧，诚望您发表高见。

译文　I dare not show off in the presence of an expert. I hope you would be kind enough to enlighten us on this matter.

译例 6　你应该大刀阔斧。

译文　You should be bold and resolute.

译例 7　敌军闹得全村鸡犬不宁。

译文　The enemy troops threw the whole village into great disorder.

译例 8　这些问题盘根错节，三言两语说不清楚。

译文　These problems are too complicated to be explained clearly in a few words.

分析　以上译例中，汉语原文都形象具体，但很难直译。在汉语中，越是具体形象的表达方式，越难在英语中找到直接对应的表达，翻译时往往用抽象的表达对其进行解释，实现意义对等。

第 3 节　合并译法

英语表达强调言简意赅，尤其在书面语中。在汉英翻译中，对一些并列的结构可以进行合并翻译，有助于译文的简洁和流畅。合并译法主要包括动词合并、形容词合并和副词合并。

3.1　动词合并

汉语是"动态"的语言，动词使用比较多；英语相对偏"静态"，动词使用相对较少，名词或名词短语使用较多。汉英翻译时，往往可以对一些并列结构的动词进行合并，既做到表达的简洁，又有助于表达的地道。如：

译例 1 不少企业积极承担社会责任，帮助当地兴医办学、铺路建桥，树立了良好形象。

译文　Many of them have shouldered social responsibilities and established a good image by helping local communities build hospitals, schools, roads and bridges.

分析　"兴医办学、铺路建桥"包含四个动宾结构：兴医、办学、铺路和建桥。假设贴字面翻译，英语也用四个动词加四个宾语，译文将显得拖沓冗长，因此翻译时可以将四个动词合并为一个动词 build，译为 build hospitals, schools, roads and bridges。

译例 2 在中国我们每到一个城市，就逛大街、逛商店、逛公园、上剧场、下饭馆。

译文　In every Chinese city, we got into the streets, shops, parks, theaters and restaurants.

分析　"逛大街、逛商店、逛公园、上剧场、下饭馆"有五个动宾结构，这五个动词可以合并译为 get into，再接五个宾语 the streets, shops, parks, theaters and restaurants。动词合并的关键是能否找到一个能同时和后面所有宾语搭配的动词。

译例 3 2008 年四川汶川大地震后，灾区电话无法接通，手机信号中断。

译文　After the devastating Wenchuan earthquake in China in 2008, both telephones and mobile phones failed to work.

分析　"灾区电话无法接通，手机信号中断"中的"无法接通"和"信号中断"可以合并译为 failed to work。其实，这里不是说一定要合并，但合并确实会使表达更加简洁，而且通过减少动词的使用，译文显得更加"静态"、地道。

译例 4 中国和欧盟是两大战略力量，肩负推动全球经济发展、促进人类文明进步、维护世界和平的崇高使命。

译文　As two strategic forces in the world, China and European Union shoulder the lofty mission to promote global economic development, peace and the progress of human civilization.

分析　翻译"推动全球经济发展、促进人类文明进步、维护世界和平"时，将三个动词"推动、促进、维护"合并译为 promote。假设直译为"boost world economy, promote the progress of civilization and uphold global peace"，则要逊色一些。此外，由于"全球经济发展"和"世界和平"可译为 global economic development 和 global peace，都可用

global 修饰，而"人类文明"的修饰语为 human，"经济发展"和"世界和平"并列关系更近一些，故翻译时调整语序，使"经济发展"和"和平"共用一个形容词修饰，"人类文明进步"放在最后翻译。

上述并列结构中，动词合并翻译是理想的做法。但需要注意的是，动词合并翻译必须确保动词能够和后面所有宾语搭配，否则还得分译。动词合并翻译的主要问题是，很多学生找不到一个可以和后面所有宾语搭配的动词。

3.2　形容词和副词的合并

并列结构中的修饰成分，也可以根据具体情况进行合并翻译，做到译文的简洁，但合并必须以保持原意为前提，不可改变原文的意思。

译例 5　我们又一次领受了他那广博的知识、丰富的经验和无穷的智慧。

译文　He once again imparted to us his great knowledge, experience and wisdom.

分析　原文中，"广博""丰富"和"无穷"分别修饰"知识""经验"和"智慧"。翻译时可以将三个修饰语合译为 great，用一个形容词修饰三个名词，意义和原文一致。和动词合并类似，形容词合并翻译的关键在于找到一个能同时修饰后面所有名词，且不违背原意的单词。

译例 6　美国不应指望一方面在全世界近乎疯狂地围追堵截中国、毫无底线地造谣污蔑中国、肆无忌惮地干涉中国内政，另一方面又要求中国在双边和全球事务中给予美方理解和支持。

译文　While unscrupulously containing and smearing China around the world, and meddling in China's domestic affairs, the United States should not demand unrealistically that China show understanding and support the United States in bilateral and global affairs.

分析　原文三个副词"近乎疯狂地""无底线地""肆无忌惮地"分别修饰"围追堵截""造谣污蔑"和"干涉"。这三个副词都是表达"过分或没有底线"的意思，带有很强的贬义，翻译时可以合并为一个副词 unscrupulously，即可传达原文的意思，不需要分别译成三个副词。

真题译·注·评

◆◆◆ 译文对照 ◆◆◆

[1]《孙子兵法》历来被尊为兵经，号称兵学鼻祖。英美法日俄等许多国家都有[2]《孙子兵法》译本，广为流传，得到一致好评，享有崇高地位。（中南民族大学·真题）

The Art of War has been esteemed as a classic military work, the earliest one all over the world. There is a translation of this book in many countries, including Britain, America, France, Japan and Russia. It enjoys great popularity and widespread praise, holding a position of great importance in these countries.

日本企业家最早将《孙子兵法》用于经济活动、企业管理，将军事战略原则用于企业战略、企业竞争，使日本经济在战后一片废墟上迅速崛起，成为世界经济大国。

It was Japanese entrepreneurs that first applied the methodology in the book to business activities and corporate management. They used the strategic principles in corporate strategy and competition, helping Japan grow rapidly into a global economic giant in post-war ruins.

今天东南亚成为经济增长最快地区，欧美各国经济增长速度滞后。欧美各国研究[3]这一经济现象时，发现[4]它与中华文化背景紧密相关。从此，世界上又掀起一个研究《孙子兵法》的热潮。不但将《孙子兵法》的原则用于最现代化的海湾战争，同时将它用于世界各国企业之间的经济战。

Today, the Southeast Asia boasts the rapidest economic growth while the western countries become sluggish in their economic development. Studies by the western countries on the economic phenomenon suggested that the achievements of Southeast Asia were closely related to Chinese cultural background. After that, there emerged another craze for studying *The Art of War*, and the military principles in it were not only used in the most modern Gulf War, but also in business competition among the enterprises of different countries.

《孙子兵法》是世界文化史上的一朵奇葩，孙武是中华民族引以为傲的杰出的军事家。

The Art of War is a unique and great book in the history of the global culture, and its author Sun Tzu is an outstanding military strategist of whom all Chinese people are proud.

1　翻译首先要理解好原文，"兵经"即"兵学经典作品"或"军事学经典作品"，"鼻祖"是"最早"的意思。

2　汉语原词可以不断重复，而英语尽量避免重复。此句《孙子兵法》译为"this book"即可，不用重复 *The Art of War*。

3　"这一经济现象"指的是前文讲的"今天东南亚成为经济增长最快地区，欧美各国经济增长速度滞后"，汉英翻译时注意识别指代关系。

4　"它"指的是"今天东南亚成为经济增长最快地区"，注意代词的指代。

◆◆◆ 知识点评 ◆◆◆

（1）增补文化背景

文化背景信息的处理是汉英翻译中的常见问题。有些关于中国文化背景的知识对英语国家读者来说是陌生的，直译可能会导致其感到困惑，影响对译文的理解。汉英翻译时，对一些重要的文化背景可以给出相关的解释，从而更好地达到交流的效果。

译例 1　《孙子兵法》是世界文化史上的一朵奇葩，孙武是中华民族引以为傲的杰出的军事家。

译文　The Art of War is a unique and great book in the history of the global culture, and its author Sun Tzu is an outstanding military strategist of whom all Chinese people are proud.

分析　孙武，是《孙子兵法》的作者，但外国读者一般不知道这个背景，假设直译名字，外国读者会对突然出现一个陌生名字感到困惑，因此增补 its author，表明其身份，更清晰地传达原文信息。

译例 2　⑩中国美术馆是以收藏、研究、展示中国近现代至当代艺术家作品为重点的国家艺术博物馆，是新中国成立以后的国家文化标志性建筑。

译文　National Art Museum of China mainly collects, studies, and displays artworks of modern and contemporary China. It has been a cultural landmark since the founding of People's Republic of China in 1949.

分析　译文是面向外国读者，不是本国读者，这是翻译的出发点。如果"新中国"直译为 new China，英语读者可能会感到困惑：What is new China？我们都知道"新中国"的含义，指的是 1949 年成立的中华人民共和国，但外国读者缺乏这种背景知识，因此翻译时补充"新中国"的文化背景，将其译为：since the founding of People's Republic of China in 1949。且原文是中国美术馆的对外宣传，是正式的材料，这种补充更显得有必要。

译例 3　⑩广州又称"羊城"，是祖国的南大门，早在秦汉时期就是繁华的都会。

译文　Guangzhou, also known as Canton, lies in the southern part of China. The city became a prosperous metropolis in Qin and Han dynasties more than 2,000 years ago.

分析　秦汉是中国历史上的两个朝代，中国人对它们都有大致的了解。但是，一般的外国读者并不了解这两个朝代。原文"早在秦汉时期"凸显了时间的久远，因此有必要增补和这两个朝代相关的时间信息。译文增译"more than 2,000 years ago"，有效地传达了"时间久远"的内涵意义。如果不增补文化背景，外国读者可能领会不到原文想要表达的广州悠久、光辉的历史。

（2）淡化文化背景

汉英翻译时，有些次要的文化背景或者对于读者来说不重要的背景信息，可以淡化处理，有时甚至可以省译。

译例 4 拓 从小我就生长在农村，很少人会去重视知识的重要性，加上我们**乡**就只有唯一一所高中，升学率很低。（合肥工业大学·真题）

译文 I grew up in the countryside where few were aware of the importance of knowledge. And then there was only one high school in my hometown, so most students would hardly have the chance to study further there.

分析 "乡"是中国县或区以下的农村基层行政区划单位，英语国家一般没有和"乡"对应的单位，所以找不到直接对应的表达方式。但是，在原文中，"乡"并不是读者关注的重点信息，也不会对读者理解产生大的影响，因此可以淡化处理，译为 hometown。如果增补文化背景信息，对不重要的信息解释一番，读者可能会感到费解且抓不住重点。

译例 5 拓 刘氏子者，少任侠，有胆气，**常客游楚州淮阴县**，交游多市井恶少。邻人王氏有女，求聘之，王氏不许。《太平广记》

译文 The young son of the Lius was a daring tough who had spent most of his adulthood in Huaiyin County associating with the town thugs. Once, he took a fancy to the daughter of the Wangs, his next-door neighbor. But when he asked for her hand, he was flatly turned down.（张光前 译）

分析 "楚州"是中国古代一个地名。在原句中，只是一个地点概念，关于它的信息不重要，并不是读者关注的重点。此外，其后还有一个地点"淮阴"，因此可以省译"楚州"，保留县名即可，不影响传递原文意思。

文化背景信息是增补还是淡化是由该信息的重要性决定的。如果文化背景对读者理解译文来讲是必要的信息，就应该补充相关信息；如果文化背景信息不重要，对读者理解译文没有影响，就可以淡化处理或省译。

句子翻译

第4讲 汉英语言对比

第1节 竹状与树状

汉语习惯按时间顺序或逻辑顺序逐层展开，层与层之间往往由逗号隔开，结构犹如竹子，句子之间的语法关系和逻辑关系注重隐性连贯，少用甚至不用关系词。而英语注重显性衔接，词组与词组、句子与句子之间的结构关系和逻辑联系一般交代得十分清楚。英语可以通过介词、关系代词、关系副词、连接词等从形态上维系句内和句间的各种关系。因此英语句子结构呈树状，分叉处由各类关系词衔接。汉英翻译时，要注意"竹状"到"树状"的转化，从而确保译文更为地道。

译例 1 男孩哭得心都快碎了，当我问及他时，他说饿极了，有两天没吃了。

译文 The boy, who was crying as if his heart would break, said, when I spoke to him, that he was very hungry because he had had no food for two days.

分析 上例中，汉语原文按照事件发生的时间先后顺序节节展开，先描述"男孩哭"，接着描述男孩哭的状态"哭得都快心碎了"，然后"当我问及他时"，男孩解释哭的原因"饿极了，有两天没吃了"，虽无关系词衔接，但语意依然连贯，结构紧凑，典型的汉语"竹状"特征。而英语句子善用关系词衔接。因此，在翻译时，英语译文将"the boy said that..."看作句子的主干，其中 that 引导的宾语从句是译文的第一个分支；第一个分支里还包含次分支——when 引导的时间状语从句（男孩说话的时间）和 because 引导的原因状语从句（解释男孩说饿极了的原因）。此外，译文令 who 引导定语从句作第二个分支，描述男孩的状态（哭）；该分支又令 as if 引导次分支，描述男孩哭的程度（哭得心都快碎了）。整体的译文呈"树状"特征，长满枝节，枝叶繁茂。

译例 2 由于距离远，又缺乏交通工具，使农村与外界隔绝，而这种隔绝，又由于通讯工具不足而变得更加严重。

译文 The isolation of the rural area, because of distance and lack of transport facilities, is compounded by the paucity of communication tools.

分析 汉语原文按照逻辑顺序逐层展开，先说"距离远和缺乏交通工具导致农村与外界隔绝"，再进一步说"这种隔绝现在变得更加严重"。首先，根据意群，可以在"使农村与外界隔绝"处断句，把句子分成前后两个部分。第一部分讲述导致"隔绝"这一结果，第二部分强调"现在隔绝更加严重"。相比第一部分，第二部分信息更加重要。因此，可以将"这种隔绝变得更加严重"作为该句的核心意思，翻译时作为"树状"译文的躯干，"由于距离远，又缺乏交通工具"作为第一个分支，作原因状语解释导致"隔绝"的原因，由 because of 引导；"又由于通讯工具不足"作第二个分支，解释"这种隔绝变得更加严重"的原因，由 by 引导。因此，汉译英时，应先分析原文的逻辑顺序，将逻辑上最重要的部分确定为译文的"树干"，再长"枝叶（汉语原文逻辑次要的部分）"。这样，就能克服两种语言的结构束缚，写出符合目的语习惯的译文。

译例 3 40 多年来，武汉杂技在继承了传统杂技的基础上，大胆吸收其他姊妹艺术之长，运用多种艺术手段将布景、灯光、道具、美术融为一体，使杂技表演成为综合性的表演艺术。

译文 For 40 years, based on traditional acrobatic techniques, Wuhan acrobatics has absorbed bravely the strong points of other sister arts and mixed scenery, lighting, props and fine art together by using all kinds of artistic methods so that the acrobatic performance becomes a comprehensive art of performance.

分析 原文讲的是武汉杂技在过去 40 多年的变化，按时间先后顺序展开，先"继承"，再"吸收……将……融为一体"，最后"杂技表演成为综合性的表演艺术"。本句的主题是"武汉杂技"，翻译时可以用它作主语，"吸收"作第一个谓语动词，"将……融为一体"作并列谓语动词，其他成分处理为译文的"枝叶"。第一个分支"在继承了传统杂技的基础上"可用过去分词短语 based on 引导；"运用多种艺术手段"可译为 by 引导的方式状语；"使杂技表演成为综合性的表演艺术"是前面做法的目的，可以译为 so that 引导的目的状语从句。

译例 4 中国在自己发展的历史长河中，形成了优良的历史文化传统。这些传统，随着时代变迁和社会进步获得扬弃和发展。

译文 In the prolonged course of development, China has formed its fine historical and cultural traditions, which have been either developed or discarded with the changes of the times and social progress.

分析 该译例原文按逻辑顺序逐层展开，第一层介绍"中国形成了优良的历史文化传统"，第二层对"这些传统"的情况进行介绍。第二层的主语"这些传统"指代第一层中的宾语"优良的历史文化传统"，故翻译时，可以将第一层的主干处理为译文的主干；将第一层中的"在自己发展的历史长河中"作为第一个分支，处理为 In 引导的短语作状语；将第二层作为第二个分支，处理为 which 引导的定语从句；且第二个分支也包含一个次分支"随着时代变迁和社会进步"，处理为 with 引导的伴随状语。由此，生成一个典型的英语"树状"句子。

第 2 节　意合与形合

意合与形合是汉语和英语的一个重要区别。汉语重意合，句子各成分之间或句子之间的结合多依靠语义的贯通，少用连接词，所以句法结构形式短小精悍。英语则重形合，语句各成分的相互结合需要连接词，以表示其结构关系。汉英翻译时，要注意汉语"意合"的特点，将原文句间隐含的逻辑关系找出，再用恰当的连接词体现出来，呈现出英语"形合"的结构。

译例 1　蜜蜂这物件，最爱劳动。广东天气好，花又多，蜜蜂一年四季都不闲着。酿的蜜多，吃的可有限。

译文　The bees are industrious. They work the whole year round, since Guangdong province boasts warm weather and plenty of flowers. Though they produce much honey, they eat only a fraction of it.

分析　"广东天气好，花又多，蜜蜂一年四季都不闲着"前后存在因果关系；"酿的蜜多，吃的可有限"前后存在让步关系。本例中，汉语不需要连词便能体现句间逻辑，但英语需要借助连词 since 和 Though 把句间的因果和转折逻辑关系体现出来，否则译文可读性将受到影响，逻辑也不清晰。

译例 2　他的肺不好，冬天易感冒。

译文　It is easy for him to catch a cold in winter because of his weak lung.

分析　汉语原文存在因果关系——因为"肺不好"，所以"冬天易感冒"。汉英翻译时用 because of 把句间因果关系体现出来。

译例 3　中国努力促进国内粮食增产，在正常情况下，粮食自给率不低于 95%。

译文　China endeavors to increase its grain production so that its self-sufficiency rate of grain under normal condition will be no less than 95 percent.

分析　汉语句间逻辑有时很明显，如上面讨论过的两个例子，但有时需要通过分析才能推出其中逻辑关系。此例中，汉语原文中的后一个分句（在正常情况下，粮食自给率不低于95%）是第一个分句（中国努力促进国内粮食增产）的目的，这种关系在汉语里是隐藏的，而在汉译英时需用显性标记 so that 表示出来，否则译文读者难以捕捉两个分句间的逻辑关系。

译例 4　世界上本没有路，走的人多了，也便成了路。

译文　Actually the earth had no roads to begin with, but when many men pass one way, a road is made.

分析　还原原文句间逻辑，可以发现原文前后分句在逻辑上存在转折关系：世界上本没有路，（但是）（当）走的人多了，也便成了路。译文用 but 表现前后的转折关系，用 when 引导时间状语从句。此外，actually 和 to begin with 的添加，也很到位，使前后逻辑衔接更为顺畅，意义更为连贯。

译例 5　**吃苦在前，享乐在后。**

译文　Be the first to bear hardships and the last to enjoy comforts.

分析　虽然汉语原文没有连接词，但显而易见，其前后属并列关系。译文通过 and 这一连接词，外显前后句间的并列关系。

　　从上面例子，我们可以看出，"意合"的汉语有时隐藏了内在的逻辑关系，汉语为母语的人不怎么费劲就能理解其意义，但在译成英语时却要适当添加一些连接词，将隐含的逻辑关系显现出来，使译文更加符合英语"形合"的表达习惯。

第 3 节　动态与静态

英语多使用名词或名词短语，呈现出相对"静态"的特点。相比之下，汉语则更偏向于"动态"，在表达中动词的使用更为频繁。因此，汉英翻译往往把汉语的动词转化为英语的其他词性，如名词、介词等，从而使译文更加符合英语的表达习惯。

译例 1　维护世界和平，促进共同发展，谋求合作共赢，是各国人民的共同愿望，也是不可抗拒的当今时代潮流。中国高举和平、发展、合作的旗帜，坚持走和平发展道路，与世界各国一道，共同致力于建设一个持久和平、共同发展的和谐世界。

译文　Universal peace, common development and win-win cooperation are the common wish of people all over the world and also an irreversible trend of our times. In this context, China, in a spirit of peace, development and cooperation, follows the path of peaceful development and works with other countries for a harmonious world of everlasting peace and common prosperity.

分析　原文中画横线的动词在译文中均没有出现。如果直译"维护世界和平，促进共同发展，谋求合作共赢"中的三个动词，动词的堆砌使用不符合英语的"静态"特点，因此英译时将原文三个动宾短语翻译为三个名词短语，此时译文意思也没有损失。"高举旗帜"若直译成英语 uphold a banner，虽然字面上看意思正确，但此处的"高举旗帜"不是指"高举"这一具体动作和"旗帜"这一具体物象，而是表示"秉着……精神"，具有象征意义。故英译时，需要突出其象征意义，而不是译为 uphold a banner 这样呈现动态动作的译文。因此，翻译时将其转化为了介词词组 in a spirit of；此外，"致力于建设"中的动词"建设"也可以省译，用介词 for 来体现其目标，译文同样"静"态。

上述译文中的动词相比汉语原文大大减少了。如果原文的每个动词都对应翻译为英语动词，虽然在语法上可以这么做，但译文会显得冗余且不够地道。

译例 2　一切爱好和平的人民都要求全面禁止核武器，彻底销毁核武器。

译文　① All peace-loving people demand that nuclear weapons should be completely prohibited and thoroughly destroyed.

② All peace-loving people demand the complete prohibition and thorough destruction of nuclear weapons.

分析　原文有三个动词"要求""禁止"和"销毁"。译文①使用了三个对应的动词，也不是说不可以接受，按一般要求也算可以了，但是比起译文②就显得不够地道，在文采上要逊色得多。英语名词或名词短语使用较多，译文②把后两个动词直接转化为名词，译文更显"静态"，而且还避开了使用宾语从句，语言表达更加简洁。

译例 3　我们可以借助专门的仪器观察到电波在传播。

译文　① We can use a special instrument and observe the electric waves travelling along.

② With the help of a special instrument we can observe the electric waves travelling along.

分析　通过分析汉语原文可知，"借助专门的仪器"为观察电波的方式，而"观察电波传播"是"借助专门的仪器"的目的，"借助"和"观察"并非并列关系。译文①虽然也使用了两个动词，在结构上和原文保持一致，但并没有准确传达原文的句间逻辑；译文②把"借助"转化为 With the help of 作方式状语，很好地表现了原文的逻辑关系，译文也更加准确，更显"静态"。

第 4 节　含蓄与直率

含蓄与直率是汉语和英语的另外一个重要区别。汉语一般先叙事，再表明自己的想法和看法，比较含蓄；而英语一般先表态，然后再说明情况或者解释为何有这样的态度，比较直率。汉英翻译时，表达顺序有时需做调整。

译例 1　**由于受到顽强抵抗，吹嘘能在数小时之内就占领战略要地的敌人，甚至还没能占领外围阵地，这一事件使我增强了信心。**

译文　I take heart from the fact that the enemy, which boasts that it can occupy the strategic point in a couple of hours, has not yet been able to take even the outlying regions, because of the stiff resistance that gets in the way.

分析　汉语原文中"由于受到顽强抵抗，吹嘘能在数小时之内就占领战略要地的敌人，甚至还没能占领外围阵地"属于叙事，"这一事件使我增强了信心"属于表态。而英语先表态再叙事，因此翻译时先表态：I take heart from the fact...，然后叙事部分以同位语从句形式直接接在 the fact 后面，译文也显得紧凑。

译例 2　**在四川西部，有一美妙去处。它背依岷山主峰雪宝鼎，树木苍翠，花香袭人，鸟声婉转，流水潺潺。它就是松潘县的黄龙。**

译文　One of the finest places in Western Sichuan is Huanglong Scenic Spot, which lies in Songpan County just beneath Xuebaoding, the main peak of the Minshan Mountain. It has lush forest, fragrant flowers, songbirds and bubbling streams.

分析　汉语在表达上一般先不表明自己的态度和目的，而是先绕个圈子，然后再点明用意，如汉语原文中"它背依岷山主峰雪宝鼎，树木苍翠，花香袭人，鸟声婉转，流水潺潺"先对圣地做一番形象的描述，使读者产生期待，然后揭开神秘面纱，指出"它就是松潘县的黄龙"；而"黄龙是四川西部的美妙去处"属于表态部分。英语往往开门见山，先表态。因此在翻译时，英语译文将表态部分提前，译为 One of the finest places in Western Sichuan is Huanglong Scenic Spot。

译例 3　**如蒙早日寄来样品或产品册，不胜感激。**

译文　It would be appreciated if samples or brochure could be soon sent to us.

分析　汉语原文的结构为条件状语在前，主句在后。而译文将表态提前，符合英语的表达习惯，开门见山，同时由 It 作形式主语，后面 if 引导的条件状语从句作真正的主语，也避免了头重脚轻，实现了句子结构平衡。

真题译·注·评

◆◆◆ **译文对比** ◆◆◆

　　中国作为 [1] 后发现代化国家，极其需要借鉴国际经验。同时，在和平崛起进程中，中国又要以自己为主，来关注和解决自己的问题。这就是说，中国的现代化一定要有中国特色。

译文 ① As a late-starter committed to modernization, China is in dire need of drawing international experience. Meanwhile, it has to focus on and address problems mainly by itself in a peaceful rise, which means its modernization must bear its own characteristics.

② As a new comer striving for modernization, China is badly in need of drawing experience from international practice. At the same time, China must rely on itself to address and resolve problems arising in the process of its peaceful rise. In other words, China's modernization must bear its own unique characteristics.

　　比如，中国将努力走出一条新的节约型道路，即 [2] 有中国特色的节约方式。现在美国人均年消费石油25桶，而中国人均消费不到1桶半。如果中国人不顾自己的条件，异想天开想做起"美国梦"，那我们对能源急切需求就会给自己，同时也会给人类带来沉重的负担和无尽的麻烦。

译文 ① For example, China will work to find out a new way to save energy in a Chinese way. Now the annual oil consumption per capita in America is 25 barrels, while that in China is less than one and a half. If we Chinese want to reach the American consumption level, actually an unrealistic American dream, such an desperate energy demand will bring heavy burden and endless trouble to us and all human beings as well.

② For instance, with regard to energy issues, China is working hard to blaze a trail in energy conservation so as to shape up a China-style [3] energy-saving approach. Currently, the American per capita annual consumption of oil is 25 barrels, while that for China is no more than a barrel and a half. Should the Chinese ignore their national conditions and indulge themselves in [4] the wildest "American Dream", the nation's desperate energy demands will undoubtedly bring heavy burden and endless trouble both to the Chinese people and the humankind as a whole.

1　"后发现代化国家"在英语中没有直接对应的表达，故翻译时解释它的意思即可。"后发现代化国家"指的是现代化起步较晚的国家，可译为：a late-starter committed to modernization。

2　"有中国特色"可以译为 bear Chinese characteristics 或 in a Chinese way，翻译中可以替换使用，避免重复。

3　energy-saving 是多余表达，上文已经很明显，讲的就是能源保护，不需要重复强调。

4　原文根本没有最高级的意思，翻译时请勿随意添加信息。

又比如，在农村富余劳动力的转移上，我们将⁵逐步走出一条中国特色的城市化道路。目前，中国农村劳动力有 5 亿多人，今后 20 年大约有两亿多人要转移出来，在这个问题上，中国人不能⁶做"欧洲梦"。欧洲在近代历史上，总共有 6000 多万人走到世界各地，到处建立殖民地，改变了世界版图。21 世纪上半叶的中国人，只能在自己的国土上，通过城市和农村的精心协调发展，在城乡之间有序流动，来解决这个⁷世界级的大难题。

译文　① As for the transfer of surplus laborers in the countryside, China will also walk on a Chinese road to urbanization. At present, there are over 0.5 billion laborers in the rural areas, and in the next 20 years more than 0.2 billion will be transferred to cities. For this problem, likewise, China can't blindly copy the European way of transferring laborers to other countries. In the history of modern Europe, over 60 million Europeans went out, established colonies all over the world and changed the world map. In the first half of the 21st century, however, Chinese will have to tackle this thorny problem within its own land by well coordinating urban and rural development and guiding orderly labor flow.

② Similarly, over the matter of migration of superfluous rural labor force to the city, China is sure to gradually find out the way towards urbanization stamped with Chinese characteristics. At present, China has a labor force of more than 500 million in the countryside, about 200 million of whom are expected to be migrated to the urban areas. In modern history, Europe has seen altogether over 60 million people depart for every corner of the world to establish colonies overseas, thereby changing the map of the world. For the Chinese people in the first half of the 21st century, however, they can only tackle this formidable universal problem within its own land, firstly by carefully coordinating urban and rural development, and secondly by providing guided and orderly flow of redundant rural labor force between the countryside and the city.

◆◆◆ 知识点评 ◆◆◆

（1）忌"懒译"和"拙译"

翻译首先要理解透原文，理清其背后的意思和逻辑，然后再根据目的语的表达习惯进行翻译。对原文不加分析，表达时不考虑目的语特点，死贴字面就是"懒译"或"拙译"。

译例 1　同时，在和平崛起进程中，中国又要以自己为主，来关注和解决自己的问题。

译文　① Meanwhile, it has to focus on and address problems mainly by itself in a peaceful rise.

② At the same time, China must rely on itself to address and resolve problems arising in the process of its peaceful rise.

5　逐步走出："走出"一条道路肯定是一个过程，"逐步"属于多余的副词修饰。

6　"做'欧洲梦'"不能直译，因为英语中找不到一个动词接 dream 作宾语，表示"做梦"的意思。翻译时可以对其进行解释，根据下文可以得知"欧洲梦"指的是欧洲向其他国家转移劳动力。

7　世界级的大难题："世界级"和"大"意义重复，省译一个。

分析 译文②即典型的"拙译"，既没有分析汉语原文的特点，也没有考虑英语表达习惯，有几个明显的问题："在和平崛起进程中"的"进程"属于动词范畴词，可以省译；"中国"不用翻成 China，用代词 it 即可，尽量避免原词重复；"以自己为主"译成介词短语 by itself 即可，可以不用 rely on 这一动词短语；译文 address 和 resolve 语义重复，均指"解决"；arising 多余，没有实质意义，因为 problems in the process of her peaceful life 已经包含了 arising 之意。译文②句子使用了 rely on，address，resolve 和 arising 四个动词性质的表述，动词太多，不符合英语的"静态"特征。

译例 2 比如，中国将努力走出一条新的节约型道路，即有中国特色的节约方式。现在美国人均年消费石油 25 桶，而中国人均消费不到 1 桶半。如果中国人不顾自己的条件，异想天开想做起"美国梦"，那我们对能源急切需求就会给自己，同时也会给人类带来沉重的负担和无尽的麻烦。

译文 ① If we Chinese want to reach the American consumption level, actually an unrealistic American dream, such an desperate energy demand will bring heavy burden and endless trouble to us and all human beings as well.

② Should the Chinese ignore their national conditions and indulge themselves in the wildest "American Dream", the nation's desperate energy demands will undoubtedly bring heavy burden and endless trouble both to the Chinese people and the humankind as a whole.

分析 "异想天开想做起'美国梦'"暗含了"不顾自己的条件"的意义，所以"不顾自己的条件"可省去不译，但译文②并没有省译，只是一味地贴字面翻译。此外，根据前文可知，"我们对能源急切需求"指达到"美国人均年消费石油 25 桶"这一需求，demand 应该用单数，译文② demands 用复数形式，指两个或多个需求，和前文表述不一致，没有准确传达原文信息。由此可见，翻译时大家应注意汉语的隐含指代关系，在英译时注意辨别名词单复数的使用。

(2) 给译文消肿

要做到简洁，首先要省译一些语境中包含的意思和重复的意思，其次要尽量用简化的表达，不要啰嗦。

译例 3 又比如，在农村富余劳动力的转移上，我们将逐步走出一条中国特色的城市化道路。

译文 ① As for the transfer of surplus laborers in the countryside, China will also walk on a Chinese road to urbanization.

② Similarly, over the matter of migration of superfluous rural labor force to the city, China is sure to gradually find out the way towards urbanization stamped with Chinese characteristics.

分析 根据我国国情而言，"农村富余劳动力转移"指的就是由农村转移到城市，故译文②中 to the city 属于语境包含的意思；"走出"是一个过程，也包含了"逐步"这一意味，故 gradually 是多余的副词修饰，两处皆可以省译；且译文②对"中国特色的城市化道路"的翻译 the way towards urbanization stamped with Chinese characteristics 虽与原文对应，但过于冗长，可以改译为 a Chinese way to urbanization。大家在翻译过程中也要尽量避免逐字逐句翻译导致的诸多问题。

第 5 讲　一般句子翻译技巧

第 1 节　断句法

断句是汉英翻译的重要技巧。断句，也叫分译或拆句，就是对原文进行层次划分，分别译成两句或更多的句子。当汉语原文是一个较长的流水句时，英语很难用一个句子与之对应，故可进行断句分译处理。

流水句是汉语句子的一大特点。流水句包含若干较短的小句，各小句之间没有关联词连接，如行云流水般，因此而得名。遇到较长的流水句，需要理清各部分之间的语义关系，拆解后译出。

1.1　意群断句

汉语中一个句子往往包含几个分句，用逗号隔开。这时断句的依据就是看它包含几层意思或有几个意群。如：

译例 1　中华民族繁衍在中国这块土地上，各民族相互融合，// 具有强大的凝聚力，形成了崇尚统一、维护统一的价值观念。

译文　The Chinese people have lived and multiplied on this land, where all ethnic groups have been highly integrated. In the process of the integration, they have forged strong cohesiveness among themselves, and have developed the values of cherishing and safeguarding unity for their country.

分析　原文包含四个分句，可划分为两层意思。前两个分句均是对中华民族的介绍，意义更为紧密，是第一个意群；而后两个分句是第一层意思产生的结果，归为第二个意群。所以翻译时，根据汉语意群，在第二个分句末尾断开，将原文分译为两句话。在第一句话后加 In the process of the integration 是为了译文的衔接和意义的连贯。

译例 2　中国美术馆现收藏各类美术作品 10 万余件，以 19 世纪末至今中国艺术名家和各时期代表作品为主，// 构成中国现代以来的美术发展序列，// 兼有部分古代书画和外国艺术作品，同时也包括丰富的民间美术作品。

译文　National Art Museum of China has a collection of more than 100,000 pieces of art, and most of them are masterpieces by outstanding artists or representative works of different periods created since the end of the 19th century. All of these works represent the historical development of modern Chinese art. The museum also collects some ancient Chinese paintings and calligraphy, foreign artworks and numerous Chinese folk art works.

分析　原文包含五个分句，可划分为三层意思。前两个分句介绍美术馆的收藏情况，可以看作第一个意群；第三个分句从另外一个角度对这些作品进行介绍，归为第二个意群；最后两个分句介绍美术馆的其他收藏，归为第三个意群。译文按意群将原文分译成三个句子，内容层次分明。

1.2　主语变化处断句

汉语复句中，常常会出现多个不同的主语，英译时可以在主语变换处断句。如：

译例3 她隔窗望去，突然发现有只小船停泊在河边，// 船里有位船夫睡得正香。

译文 Looking through the window, she suddenly spotted a boat moored to the bank. In it there was a boatman fast asleep.

分析 原句有两个主语，即"她"和"船夫"，分句之间仅用逗号隔开，这正是汉语的典型特征。英译时可以在第二个主语前断开。

译例4 国家在大力发展农村经济，// 我也期待家乡环境的改善，也相信很快就会有大的变化，// 但这些事也让我思考，我们是否应该在文化价值观方面，做出相应的指点和引导呢？

（北京外国语大学·真题）

译文 The government is vigorously developing the rural economy. I also expect improvements in my village, and I know there will soon be many changes. Yet these changes make me wonder whether we should provide some guidance and education on cultural values.

分析 原文有三个主语，即"国家""我"和"这些事"，翻译时在主语变换处断句，分译成三个句子表达原文的意思。

1.3　总分衔接处断句

汉语有些句子先总说后分述，英译时可以先在总分衔接处断句，然后进行翻译。

译例5 事实上，人类正处于极端天气的适应期，// 炎热的酷暑、狂暴的飓风、刺骨的严寒以及滔天的洪水近乎成了"常客"，风调雨顺已被视为"奢侈品"。

译文 Actually, humans are in a stage of adapting to extreme weather patterns. High temperatures, ferocious hurricanes, icy cold and big floods seem to have become regular visitors to the earth, while sound or agreeable weather has become rare, even "luxury".

分析 原文先说明总体情况，即"人类正处于极端天气的适应期"，再说明此类极端天气的具体表现，英译时可在总分衔接处断开。

译例6 中国高度重视互联网发展，// 自21年前接入国际互联网以来，我们按照积极利用、科学发展、依法管理、确保安全的思路，加强信息基础设施建设，发展网络经济，推进信息惠民。

译文 The Chinese government attaches great importance to the Internet development. Since the introduction of the Internet 21 years ago, China, under the guideline of active utilization, sound development, law-based governance and guaranteed security, has improved the IT infrastructure and developed cyber-economy to benefit people's life.

分析 "中国高度重视互联网发展"是总说，接下来介绍中国政府为此做了哪些事情，是分述。总分衔接处断句是一种比较明显的断句标记方式，比较易于掌握。

第 2 节　合句法

　　汉语多短句、小句，而英语长句较多。因此，汉英翻译时，有时可以把两个或两个以上的汉语短句翻译成一个英语长句，从而使译文结构更紧凑、意思更连贯、更加符合目的语特点，这种翻译方法便是"合句法"。

2.1　提炼同一主题

译例 1　古人所谓的"一目十行"，只是修辞上的夸张。"一目十行"只有两种情形：一是那本书不值得读，二是那个人不会读书。（广东外语外贸大学·真题）

译文　The ancient saying "read ten lines at one glance" is just a rhetorical hyperbole and people do that only when the book is not worth reading or they themselves have no idea of how to read a book.

分析　原文第一、二句话都是对"一目十行"进行说明。在英语中，同一个主题下的相关信息往往可以使用并列结构来表达。译文用 and 连接前后两个句子，衔接顺畅、结构紧凑，符合英语的表达习惯。

译例 2　经得起这批特殊读者再三精读的书，想必是佳作。经得起他们读上几十年几百年的书，一定成为经典了。（北京语言大学·真题）

译文　Any book repeatedly read by these special readers must be a good work, and if read by them for decades or for hundreds of years, it must be a classic one.

分析　原文第一句话的主题是"书"，第二句话的主题也是"书"。因此，英译时，可以用 book 作主语，再用 and 连接前后两句，使之合成一句话。

译例 3　旧历新年快来了。这是一年中的第一件大事。除了那些负债过多的人，大家都热烈欢迎这个佳节的到来。

译文　The Lunar New Year is fast approaching, the first event of the year, and everyone, except those who owe heavy debts, is enthusiastically looking forward to it.

分析　原文有三个句号，可以划分成三个意群。第二个句子是对旧历新年进行解释，所以在翻译时，可以将第一个句子作为主句，第二个句子作为同位语补充说明第一个句子。第三个句子和前面内容关系紧密，但主语不同，可以作为并列句处理，由 and 连接。关于第三个句子的翻译，可以先确定句子主干"大家都热烈欢迎这个佳节的到来"，再用 except 作为介词引出"那些负债过多的人"。原文是三个结构零散的独立小句，经过以上处理，译文合成了一个语意连贯、逻辑清晰、结构紧凑的长句。

2.2 进行信息重组

本书第 1 讲【真题译·注·评】中的知识点评部分也有提及为使译文流畅、地道而进行信息重组的翻译方法。此外，在汉英翻译中，有时为将诸多汉语短句合并译为一个英语长句，也需在保留原文意义的前提下，打破原文结构，对信息进行重组。如：

译例 4 旅行团从澳大利亚乘飞机到达香港，然后坐火车到中国各地游览。这次趣味盎然的旅行长达数千里。

译文 Flying from Australia to Hong Kong, the tourist group then embarked on a fascinating journey spanning thousands of miles through China by train.

分析 在句意不变的前提下，原文两句话可以灵活重组为以 "旅行团" 为主语的一句话：旅行团从澳大利亚飞到香港，然后乘火车经历了一次长达数千里、趣味盎然的中国之旅。翻译该句时，可以将 "从澳大利亚飞到香港" 处理为现在分词引导的状语；将 "长达数千里" 作为后置定语修饰 journey 即可，不用单独成句，这样译文更加简洁、精炼。

译例 5 我们北外网院已经成为一个品牌。教育部的赞扬、社会的认同、成功的国际合作，以及无需做广告，是我们的回报。

译文 Our efforts have given the Institute of Online Education in Beijing Foreign Studies University (BFSU) a recognizable name, so we do not have to advertise, and other rewards include praise from the Ministry of Education, recognition from the public, and successful cooperation with international partners.

分析 通过分析汉语原文，可以得出，"成为品牌" 和 "无需做广告" 关系更为密切，后者为前者的结果，而 "教育部的赞扬、社会的认同、成功的国际合作" 和 "成为品牌" 一起作为北外网院努力的回报。故翻译时信息重组，把 "无需做广告" 提前，作 "成为品牌" 的结果状语；将 "教育部的赞扬、社会的认同、成功的国际合作" 和 "成为品牌" 合并处理，用 and 连接。经过上述处理，原文两个句子合译成一个关系紧密、结构紧凑、语意连贯的英语长句。

第 3 节 省译法

汉英翻译中，译文要做到言简意赅，遣词造句应尽可能做到表达简练，去掉多余的、可有可无的表达。很多同学用英语把意思表达出来似乎不存在很大障碍，但要表达简洁就不是那么简单。中国学生翻译时受到汉语原文影响，译文往往啰嗦冗长，从而影响译文的地道以及可读性。

3.1 避免多余从句

相对单词来说，从句表达的意思更为复杂。当原文意思简单，单词就可以传达意思的时候，并不需要用从句来表达，这样可以避免译文冗长。学生译文中，定语从句多余的现象尤其普遍。如：

译例 1 作为一个母亲，我在**顽皮的**女儿面前没有权威。

译文 ① As a mother, I got no authority over my daughter who is a naughty girl.

② I got no authority over my naughty daughter.

分析 原文中"顽皮的"一词可以直接译为前置定语 naughty 修饰 daughter 即可，不需要大费周章将其译成定语从句。且 As a mother 的意思已经暗含在后半句当中，不需要重复翻译。因此，译文②更好。

译例 2 变化之一是**电脑出现了**，这在世界的每个角落都可以看到。

译文 ① One of the changes is that the computer emerged, which can nearly be seen in every corner of the world.

② One of the changes is the emergence of computers in every corner of the world.

分析 译文①使用了 that 引导的表语从句描述变化，又用了一个非限制性定语从句"..., which can nearly be seen in every corner of the world"来进一步解释这种变化的普遍性。译文①传达了原文的意思，但它表述复杂，不够地道，因为英语倾向于使用更简洁的结构。译文②采用了名词"emergence"来表达原文中的动词"出现"，并将整个句子简化为一个简单句。译文②这种翻译更加地道，因为它遵循了英语倾向于使用名词和"静态"表达的习惯。同时，它也避免了使用复杂的从句结构，使句子更加简洁明了。

译例 3 许多大学为那些**愿意参加并且有资格参加**的学生提供第二外语课程作为选修课。

译文 ① In many universities, second foreign languages are provided as optional courses for students who are willing as well as qualified to take them.

② Many universities provide an optional second foreign language course for willing and qualified students.

分析 一般来说，英语中定语尽量前置，除非信息复杂，前置不了，才会使用后置定语。"愿意参加并且有资格参加的学生"，可以直接译为：willing and qualified students，不需要像译文①一样使用定语从句。因此，译文②更好。

译例 4　这八年是国家经济实力显著增强的时期。

译文　① These eight years constitutes a period in which the national economic strength has increased.
② In these eight years the national economy has grown stronger.

分析　原文本身就是一个简单句，译文②同样为简单句结构，言简意赅地表达了原文的意思，而译文①运用了由 in which 引导的定语从句，反而将简单的句子复杂化，译文显得更为啰嗦，不够利落。因此，译文②更好。

译例 5　但一部小说开掘得深不深，艺术和思想是否有过人之处，的确不在题材大小。

译文　① But whether a novel is deeply explored, or whether its artistry and idea are excellent, do not depend on whether it has a grand theme.
② But the depth of a novel, or the excellence of its artistry and idea, does not depend on whether it has a grand theme.

分析　译文①和原文字面对应，用两个主语从句对应汉语原文的两个句子，虽然在语法上可以接受，但不够简练。译文②利用英语多用名词短语的特点造句，非常地道，用两个短语翻译原文的两个句子，尽管形式简化，但意义并没有损失。

　　汉英翻译中，对于简单信息，应尽量避免使用从句以及表达复杂化，但不是说不用从句或从句不好。其实，是否用从句是由信息复杂程度决定的，当单词或短语没法传达原文意思的时候，就要用到从句。如：

译例 6　19 世纪中叶以后，由于列强的野蛮侵略和封建统治的无能，中华民族陷入了丧权辱国、民不聊生的悲惨境地。

译文　Since the 1850s, China had been reduced by foreign invasion and feudal incompetence to a dire situation where the sovereignty was violated, the nation was humiliated and people lived in extreme poverty.

分析　原文中，"丧权辱国、民不聊生的"作定语修饰"悲惨境地"，定语较为复杂，用单词或短语作前置定语没法表达，因此翻译时可以灵活转化为 where 引导的后置定语从句。总而言之，从句对应相对复杂的单词或短语表达不了的信息。

3.2　避免重复表达

　　汉语中存在大量的重复表达，往往在表达完一个意思后，又从另外一个角度对表达过的意思进行重复，而英语不喜欢对同一个意思重复表达。汉英翻译时，为了符合目的语的表达习惯，往往需要省译汉语重复的信息，使译文更简洁。

译例 7　我们要十分关心年度计划的编制工作，不能对此不闻不问。

译文　① We should pay close attention to the formulation of annual plans and should not neglect it.
② We should pay close attention to the formulation of annual plans.

译例 8　要保持警惕，决不掉以轻心。

译文　① We must maintain our vigilance and never lose our guard.
② We must maintain our vigilance.

译例 9 财政开支应按轻重缓急安排，<u>不应当主次不分</u>。

译文 ① Financial expenditures should be based on priority, and should not be spent haphazardly.

② Financial expenditures should be based on priority.

分析 以上三个译例，画线部分均和前面的分句语义重复。例如，译例 7 中，"十分关心"和"不能对此不闻不问"意义重叠，既然表达了"十分关心"肯定不会"不闻不问"，翻译前半部分即可。意义重复在汉语中非常普遍，但英语不喜欢重复，故汉英翻译时要注意识别汉语重复的信息，进行省译。

3.3 秉持精简达意

译文不仅要避免多余的从句和语义的重复，译文意思还要尽量做到清楚明了，避免晦涩难懂或意思不清晰，以更好地达到交流的目的。

译例10 她住在一个有六个家庭成员的美国家庭，夫妇都是律师，<u>四个小孩最大的上高中，最小的上小学</u>。（北京外国语大学·真题）

译文 ① She lived in an American family of six members, with the couple both lawyers and four boys old enough to attend school, with the eldest in high school and the youngest in primary school.

② She lived in an American family. The parents were both lawyers and the four boys were attending primary to high school.

分析 原文中"四个小孩最大的上高中，最小的上小学"是典型的汉语描述特征，有语义联系（暗含范围关系，即"四个孩子的学段是从小学到高中"）但又结构零散，翻译时需考虑目的语的语言特点。译文①中，第一个 with 引导独立主格，后面还有一个 with 引导的短语对前面的 four boys 进行解释说明，结构重复、零散，整体较为冗长。译文①虽然也传达了原文信息，但由于其结构零散，译文读起来不够顺畅；语句冗长也致使意思不够简洁明了。相反，译文②将其翻译为 the four boys were attending primary to high school，语法正确；仅用一个 primary to high school 短语就再现了原文的范围关系，简洁明了，且整体意义并无缺损。

北京外国语大学的李长栓教授在其著作《非文学翻译理论与实践》中列举了一个极具说服力的例子。例句如下：

① Our lack of knowledge about local conditions precluded determination of committee action effectiveness in fund allocation to those areas in greatest need of assistance.

② Because we knew nothing about local conditions, we could not determine how effectively the committee had allocated funds to areas that most needed assistance.

分析 句子①用了大量的抽象名词，且逻辑不清晰，读者要费很大劲才能理解其意思，也可能根本读不懂。第二个句子不仅用词和句式简单，逻辑也很清晰，意思一目了然。通过以上两个例子对比分析，我们要知道译文表达要尽量清楚明了，不要复杂化。毕竟，"言简意赅"是简明英语的基本原则之一。

第 4 节　转换法

转换法也是汉英句子翻译较常采用的一种翻译方法。由于汉、英两种语言分属不同的语系，因此在翻译过程中，为了使译文符合目的语的表达习惯，需对原文进行相应转换，主要包括词类转换、句子成分转换、句型转换和语态转换等。

词类转换，即词性转换，是指将原文的词类在翻译时转换为另一词类。例如，把名词转换为代词、形容词、动词或把动词转换成名词、形容词、副词等。句子成分转换指的是将原文句子中的某个成分在翻译时转换为另一种成分，例如，把主语转换成谓语、状语、定语、宾语、表语或把定语转换成状语、谓语、表语等。句型转换是指将原文中的句型在翻译时转换为另一句型，例如，把并列句转换成复合句，或把复合句转换成并列句，或把状语从句转换成定语从句等。语态转换则是指主、被动之间的转换。

转换法生于两种语言的异，致力于两种语言的同，恰当运用有助于译文表达地道。本节将重点分析句子成分、句型和语态层面的转换。

4.1　句子成分转换

译例 1　美国科罗拉多州等**西部地区**山火连绵不绝。

译文　Western America, including Colorado, witnessed incessant wildfires.

分析　原文描述了"美国西部地区"发生了"山火连绵不绝"这一事件，其中"美国西部地区"为地点状语。在英语中，表示"某地发生某事"时可以用地点作主语，用 see 或 witness 作谓语动词，将发生的事情作为宾语。故在翻译时，运用了转换法，将"美国西部地区"转换为主语。

译例 2　21 世纪上半叶的中国人，只能在自己的国土上，通过城市和农村的精心协调发展，在城乡之间有序流动，来解决这个世界级的大难题。

译文　In the first half of the 21st century, Chinese will have to tackle this thorny problem within its own land by well coordinating urban and rural development and guiding orderly labor flow.

分析　画线处在原文中作定语，修饰"中国人"。但在英语中，the first half of the 20th century 无法作前置定语修饰 Chinese，所以译文把它转化为时间状语，使译文符合英语语法要求。此外，状语单独翻译，用逗号隔开，也可以为后面的长句"减负"。

译例 3　自然界有各种不同的元素。

译文　There are different elements in nature.

分析　"自然界"在原文中作主语，如果把原文直译为"Nature has different elements"，在语法上虽然没有什么问题，但这样的译文是典型的汉语式思维，可能会让读者觉得蹩脚。"……有……"正确而又地道的译文是用 there be 结构翻译，故译文将原文中的主语"自然界"转换译为状语成分，置于句末。

译例 4　由于长江不断改道，在武汉地区形成了众多的湖泊。

译文　The constant change of the course of the Yangtze River in history helped form a great many lakes in the areas around Wuhan.

分析　通过分析原文句意，可以得出正是"长江不断改道"而导致后面的结果。鉴于英语多用名词或名词短语作主语，翻译时将原文原因状语"由于长江不断改道"转换译为主语 The constant change of the course of the Yangtze River，增译 helped form 凸显"长江不断改道"和"众多湖泊形成"之间的因果关系。

4.2　语态转换

译例 5　糟糕的天气和频发的自然灾害使全球深受其害。

译文　The world is afflicted by deplorable weather events and frequent natural disasters.

分析　原文是主动语态。如果直译为"Deplorable weather events and frequent natural disasters afflict the world."，则句子"头重脚轻"。由于英语多用被动语态，故翻译时，将原文的主动语态转换为被动语态，头轻脚重，符合英语的"尾重"特点。

译例 6　人是各式各样的，每一种人都可以取得最高的成就。例如，有的人从政，在这个领域里，最高成就便是成为一个伟大的政治家。同样，在艺术领域里，最高成就便是成为一个伟大的艺术家。人可能被分为不同等级，但他们都是人。（西南大学·真题）

译文　Humans are diverse and they each can make the greatest achievement in a certain field. For example, becoming a great statesman is the greatest achievement for those who engage in politics and becoming a great artist is the biggest achievement for those working in the field of art. Humans may belong to different classes, but they have one thing in common: they are humans.

分析　原文画线处是被动语态，但结合前文可知，人的不同等级是由个人职业决定的，不是外在力量导致的。如果把原文直译为"Humans are divided into different classes..."，虽然在语法上也对，但在语义方面没有上述译文准确。因为被动语态的译文暗示有一个施事主语（外在力量）使大家归属为不同的阶层，与原文表述相悖。所以，翻译时，将原文的被动语态转换译为主动语态 Humans may belong to different classes，意思传递更准确。

4.3　句型转换

译例 7　乌镇是浙江的一座古老水镇，坐落在京杭大运河畔。

译文　Wuzhen, located along the Beijing-Hangzhou Grand Canal, is an old watertown in Zhejiang province.

分析　原文是个并列句，介绍乌镇的相关情况。译文将并列句转换成复合句，由并列分句 1 作为主句，并列分句 2 作为一个从属成分（用过去分词短语来表达），最后得出上述译文。其实原文也可以直译为：Wuzhen is an old watertown in Zhejiang province and located along the Beijing-Hangzhou Grand Canal。但相对来说，译例 7 所给出的译文表达更简洁，衔接更顺畅。

译例 8　**由于素混凝土的抗剪强度很小，一般不用于制造梁。**

译文　Plain concrete, which is weak in shearing strength, is generally not used in making beams and girders.

分析　原文画线部分是状语从句，译文将其转换译为定语从句，放在句中作分隔结构。原文也可直译为 "Plain concrete is generally not used in making beams and girders, because it is weak in shearing strength."，完全符合英语的表达习惯。由此可见，翻译方法不是唯一的，句型转换有时可以提供另外一个翻译的角度或方法。

真题译·注·评

◆◆◆ **译文对比** ◆◆◆

¹我若为王，我的姓名就会改作：²"万岁"，我的每一句话都成为："圣旨"。我的意欲，我的贪念，乃至每一个幻想，都可³竭尽全体臣民的力量去实现，即使是无法实现的。我将没有任何过失，因为没有人敢说它是过失；我将没有任何罪行，因为没有人敢说它是罪行。没有人敢呵斥我，指责我，除非把我从王位上赶下来。但是赶下来，就是我不为王了。（山东大学·真题）

译文 ① If I were king, my name would be changed into Your Majesty. Every word of mine would be the imperial edict. My desires and greed would be met and each of my illusions realized through the efforts of all subjects, even though they may be unrealistic. I would commit no mistakes, for no one dares to call them a mistake; I would commit no crimes, for no one dares to call them a crime. And no one would dare to criticize or berate me unless I were removed from the throne. If removed, I would no longer be the king.

② If I were king, I would be addressed as Your Majesty. ⁴Certainly, every word of mine would be regarded as Imperial Edict. My desire, greed, even every fantasy would be satisfied by exerting all my people's strength, even if they couldn't be realized. I would have no fault because no one dared to call it fault. I would have no crimes because no one dared to call ⁵it a crime. No one dared to reproach or censure me, unless I was dislodged from the throne. But if that happened, I would not be the king.

⁶我将看见所有的人们在我面前低头、鞠躬、匍匐，连同我的尊长，我的师友，和从前曾在我面前⁷昂

---

1 "我若为王，……"是虚拟的假设，要用虚拟语气。这段文字后面内容都是以"我若为王"为前提展开，所以后面都用虚拟语气。

2 "万岁"是中国封建社会对最高统治者的称呼，直译"万岁"英语国家读者不好理解。在西方国家，对最高统治者的敬称为 Your Majesty，因此译为 Your Majesty，英语国家读者更易接受。

3 "竭尽"这一动词可以转换译为介词 through，译文更显"静态"。

4 前后并不存在强调关系，不用加 Certainly。

5 用 it 指代前面的 crimes 属于指代错误，应该用 them 指代，且后面的 a crime 应改为 crimes。

6 "我将看见"没有实质意义，可以省译，这样后面可以用现在分词短语 including...修饰前面的 all of the people；但是，如果译文中保留"我将看见"，就像第二个译文一样，后面就连接不起来。

7 "昂头阔步、耀武扬威"语意重复，故可省译，它们合在一起其实表达的就是"表现高傲，狂妄"的意思，翻译时只需把这一意义表达出来即可。

头阔步、耀武扬威的人们。我将看不见一个人的脸，所看见的只是他们的头顶或帽盔；[8] 所能够看见的脸都是谄媚的，乞求的，[9] 快乐的时候不敢笑，不快乐的时候不敢不笑，悲戚的时候不敢哭，不悲戚的时候不敢不哭的脸。我将听不见人们的真正的声音，所能听见的都是[10] 低微的，柔婉的，畏葸和娇痴的，唱小旦的声音："万岁，万岁！万万岁！"

译文　① All of the people would lower their head, bow or kneel in front of me, including my elders, teachers, friends and those who once treated me in an arrogant or haughty manner. I could hardly see any of their faces in front of them. What I could see is the top of their head or their helmets. They are flattering or begging me, so [11]sometimes in order to please me, they dare not smile when happy, or have to feign a smile when unhappy. Sometimes they also dare not cry when sad or have to cry when not sad. I would never hear their true voices, for they only utter to me "Wan Sui, Wan Sui! Wan Wansui!" in a soft, timid and sweet manner.

② I would see all of the people lower their heads, bow and prostrate themselves before me, [12]including my elders, teachers, friends and those once [13]striding proudly ahead. I would see no one's face but their heads or helmets on the heads. I could only see flattering and begging [14]faces that dared not smile when happy, while forcing themselves to smile when unhappy; and that dared not weep when sad, while forcing themselves to weep when not sad. I would hear no one's true voice. All I could hear would be small, soft, [15]frightened and innocent voice, like [16]a young female character's voice in Beijing opera, singing, Long Live!

8　所能够看见的脸都是谄媚的，乞求的。这句话的理解应该是：他们谄媚我，祈求我，是指人谄媚，而不是脸，脸不能执行谄媚和乞求的动作。如果直译为：their faces are flattering and begging me，译文则无法理解。

9　英语是形合的语言。"快乐的时候不敢笑，不快乐的时候不敢不笑，悲戚的时候不敢哭，不悲戚的时候不敢不哭的脸"和前面"所能够看见的脸都是谄媚的，乞求的"具有因果关系。正因为他们要谄媚、祈求我，才会有那些表现，所以译文增译了连词 so。

10　低微的，柔婉的，畏葸和娇痴的，唱小旦的声音。首先要理解好原文，"低微的"意为不敢大声说话，"柔婉的"意为讲话很柔，和"娇痴的"存在部分语义重复，"畏葸"即胆怯的意思，"小旦"是传统戏剧中旦角之一，涉及文化背景，直译译文读者可能没法理解，翻译时大致解释在本句中的意思即可。"小旦的声音"，应该是强调悦耳，和前面的"娇痴"有语义重复。"娇痴"和"小旦的声音"可以综合在一起，译为 sweet。

11　加 sometimes in order to please me，是为了前后衔接更加顺畅。

12　I would see all of the people lower their heads, bow and prostrate themselves before me, including my elders, teachers, friends... 一句中，including 引导分词短语不能对前面的 all of the people 进行修饰，因为 all of the people 后面有补语 lower their heads, bow and prostrate themselves before me。可以参考译文①的译法。

13　striding proudly ahead 意为"骄傲地大步往前走"，和原文意思不同，没有准确传达原文的意思。

14　faces 不能作 smile 的主语，英语中要用人作 smile 的主语。

15　frightened 修饰人，不能修饰 voice。

16　a young female character's voice in Beijing opera，英语国家读者可能根本不知道什么是京剧，无法理解译文意思。翻译一定要考虑译文的可读性，目标语读者是否能理解它的意思。

◆◆◆ 知识点评 ◆◆◆

注意译文的逻辑

汉语表达有时不够严谨，存在一些逻辑问题。对于原文有逻辑错误的地方，译文可以进行修补或纠正，从而避免给读者造成误导。

译例 1　所能够看见的脸都是谄媚的，乞求的，快乐的时候不敢笑，不快乐的时候不敢不笑，悲戚的时候不敢哭，不悲戚的时候不敢不哭的脸。

译文　They are flattering or begging me, so sometimes in order to please me, they dare not smile when happy, or have to feign a smile when unhappy. Sometimes they also dare not cry when sad or have to cry when not sad.

分析　臣子或下属谄媚国王，不一定是快乐的时候都不敢笑，也不是不快乐的时候都不敢不笑。当国王开心的时候是可以笑的，当国王不开心的时候也是可以不笑的。只是有的时候，不能和国王表现出相反的心情。所以译文增译 sometimes，使译文符合正常的逻辑。

译例 2　㊢国庆节回家，那个黄河边上的乡村，开小汽车的乡亲开始多见，虽然他们的穿衣打扮还没有太多的改变，但当我看到他们开上价值 20 多万的汽车时，我很是欣喜。

（北京外国语大学 · 真题）

译文　Over the National Day holiday, I went back to my village on the banks of the Yellow River. I noticed that though still dressed the same way as before, many villagers now drove cars, some even as costly as 200 thousand *yuan*. This made me happy.

分析　"当我看到他们开上价值 20 多万的汽车时"存在逻辑问题，不可能所有人开的都是 20 多万元的汽车。所以，译文予以调整，增译 some 以显示是部分人。

第6讲 成语之翻译

成语是人们长期以来习惯使用的、简洁精辟的词组或短语。无论是书面语还是口语都离不开成语。汉语成语言简意赅、生动形象，比一般词语有着更强的表现力。汉语成语结构稳定，绝大部分以四字格形式出现，例如：胸有成竹、兔死狐悲、调虎离山、走马观花、对牛弹琴、守株待兔等。汉英翻译中，汉语成语的处理是一个不可忽视的问题，一般有三种方法：直译、意译和套译。

第1节 直译法

当成语的比喻形象能为译文读者所接受时，就采用直译法。如：

汉语成语	英译
趁热打铁	strike the iron while it is hot
竭泽而渔	drain a pond to catch all the fish
牢不可破	to be strongly built as to be indestructible
打草惊蛇	stir up the grass to alert the snake
攻其不备	strike sb. when he is unprepared
熟能生巧	practice makes perfect
引狼入室	to bring the wolves into the house
调虎离山	to lure the tiger out of the hills
如坐针毡	on pins and needles
对牛弹琴	to play the lute to a cow

以上成语的翻译均采用直译法，不仅传达了原文意思，还保留了原文形象。直译的前提是译文对英语国家读者来说具有可读性。以上成语翻译完全可以被英语国家读者理解，如"趁热打铁"，西方国家也有这一生活体验，译为 strike the iron while it is hot 不存在理解上的障碍。

译例 1 调查有两种方法，一种是走马观花，一种是下马看花。

译文 There are two ways of making investigations: one is to look at flowers on horseback and the other is to get off your horse and look at them.

分析 "走马观花"比喻粗略地观察事物，英语 look at flowers on horseback 也可以表达同样的意思，因为坐在马背上肯定不能细看花朵；同样地，"下马看花"比喻仔细深入地观察事物，可以译为：get off your horse and look at them，能够体现出下马停留并细致观察的意思。只要可以表达原文内涵，就可以直译。

译例 2　你是知道的，咱们家所有的这些管家奶奶们，哪一位是好缠的？错一点儿她们就笑话打趣，偏一点儿她们就指桑骂槐的抱怨。《红楼梦》

译文　And you know how difficult our old stewardesses are, laughing at the least mistake and "accusing the elm while pointing at the mulberry tree" if one shows the least bias.

（杨宪益、戴乃迭 译）

分析　成语"指桑骂槐"比喻表面上骂这个人，实际上骂那个人。上述译文采用直译方法，保留原文形象 elm（榆树）和 mulberry tree（桑树），所呈现的语义与原文完全相同。其实，树的具体名称意义不大，用其他树名也可以，关键是内涵要一致。

第 2 节　意译法

很多汉语成语既不能直译，又没有既定的与之意义对应的英语成语，就要采用意译的方法，解释其含义或内涵。其实，绝大多数汉语成语的比喻形象英语国家读者都不太能理解，需要意译。直译的话，读者可能会不知所云，感到莫名其妙。例如，把"胸有成竹"译为：have a bamboo in one's stomach。肚子里怎么会有竹子？这样的译文英语国家读者根本无法理解。我们看一些成语意译的例子：

汉语成语	英译
沉鱼落雁	dazzling beauty
开门见山	come straight to the point
四面楚歌	be besieged on all sides
毛遂自荐	volunteer one's service
粗枝大叶	to be crude and careless
无孔不入	to take advantage of every weakness
扬眉吐气	to feel proud and elated
灯红酒绿	dissipated and luxurious
叶公好龙	professed love of what one really fears

译例 1 事实上，人类正处于极端天气的适应期，炎热的酷暑、狂暴的飓风、刺骨的严寒以及滔天的洪水近乎成了"常客"，风调雨顺已被视为"奢侈品"。这样的情况下，未雨绸缪才能处变不惊。

译文 Actually, humans are in a stage of adapting to extreme weather patterns. High temperatures, ferocious hurricanes, icy cold and big floods seem to have become regular visitors to the earth, while sound or agreeable weather has become rare, even "luxury". In this situation, only by preparing for future consequences can we keep composure.

分析 汉语原文中有两个成语："风调雨顺"和"未雨绸缪"，这两个成语均不宜直译。如果直译，译文读者难以理解其比喻义，所以采用意译法，解释其意义即可。"风调雨顺"，即天气好的意思，不用分开来翻译"风调"和"雨顺"，概括其意思即可，可译为：sound or agreeable weather；"未雨绸缪"，即为将来不好的事情提前做好准备，可译为：preparing for future consequences。

译例 2　现在，以互联网为代表的信息技术日新月异，引领了社会生产新变革，创造了人类生活新空间，拓展了国家治理新领域，极大提高了人类认识世界、改造世界的能力。

译文　At present, the Internet-represented information technology has been evolving constantly. It has reformed social production, brought new lifestyles and governmental work, and greatly improved people's ability to know and transform the world.

分析　"日新月异"，即不断变化、快速变化的意思。若将"日"和"月"直译，译文则无法传递原文形象背后的内涵，读者可能会不知所云。因此，可以意译为：evolve constantly 或 evolve rapidly。

译例 3　我在门前淅沥的小雨中默默站了一会，恍然大悟。便如同一个死里逃生的人，头一回觉得这栋隐没在夜雾和雨雾中的红砖瓦房，非常非常的可爱和温柔。（张抗抗《恐惧的平衡》）

译文　Still in a daze, as if snatched from death's grip, I suddenly realized how lovable, how warm was this old, familiar, red-brick building standing solidly in the darkness on this rainy night.

（朱虹 译）

分析　"死里逃生"，即从极危险的境地中逃脱，幸免于死。译文 snatched from death's grip 指"把生命从死神的手中抢过来"，不仅内涵与原文一致，而且语言同样生动、形象。

第 3 节　套译法

英语中有些既定的成语虽然和汉语成语的比喻形象不同，但意义相同。这种情况下，可以采用套译法，即直接引用英语中已有的成语。如：

汉语成语	英语成语
猫哭耗子	crocodiles' tears
掌上明珠	the apple of one's eye
小题大做	make a mountain out of a molehill
洗心革面	turn over a new leaf
骑虎难下	between the devil and the deep blue sea
挥金如土	spend money like water

译例　车速很快。走的是快车道。快得确实令人生疑。

那两人仍是一句话也不说。

我想这回完了。随身的包里还有刚从银行取出来的一笔稿费呢。

我<u>忐忑不安、心慌意乱</u>。我想对他们说停车停车我要下去，可话到嘴边却张不开口……

（张抗抗《恐惧的平衡》）

译文　The car was speeding away in the fast lane. Suspiciously fast, it seemed to me.

The two men were silent.

"Now I'm in for it," my heart sank. And I've just drawn out some royalty payments from the bank. They're right here in my purse!

I was on pins and needles. I wanted to stop the car and get out, but couldn't bring myself to say so...（朱虹 译）

分析　汉语原文讲的是女主人公一次单独打车，担心被抢劫的经历。"忐忑不安"形容心神非常不安，"心慌意乱"意思是心里着慌，乱了主意。两个成语意义重复，可以省译一个。译文的 on pins and needles 形容如坐针毡、焦虑不安的感觉，不仅非常忠实地传达了原文的意思，pins（别针）和 needles（针）这两个生活物品类的形象还给译文读者带来一种生动感和亲切感。

关于成语的翻译，最后还需强调一点，有些汉语成语的翻译方法并不是唯一的。上述译例中，"忐忑不安""心慌意乱"可以用套译法，译为 on pins and needles，也可以意译为 broke out in a cold sweat，译文也非常形象生动。再举一例，"对牛弹琴"可以意译为 address the wrong audiences，也可以直译为 play the lute to a cow，两种译法传达的是相同的信息，只是第一种译法损失了比喻形象。一般来说，能同时保留原文比喻形象和语义的翻译固然是最佳选择，但也要看语境，具体问题具体分析。如果在正式文体中，play the lute to a cow 会显得口语化，反而比不上第一个译文，因为在正式文体中，翻译力求准确、严肃，而非生动形象。

真题译·注·评

◆◆◆ **译文对比** ◆◆◆

2000 年，中国建成北斗导航试验系统，这使中国成为继美、俄之后世界上第三个拥有自主卫星导航系统的国家。

译文 ① BeiDou Navigation Satellite Demonstration System was built in 2000. This makes China, after America and Russia, the third country to have independent navigation system in the world.

② In 2000, China [1]successfully established the [2]BeiDou Satellite Navigation Experimental System (also known as BeiDou-1), making it the third country in the world, after America and Russia, to have its own navigation system.

虽然目前北斗导航系统的定位精度与 GPS 还有一定的差距，但它具备了 GPS 所没有的短报[3]通信和位置报告的功能。在没有手机信号的地方，用户也可以通过[4]该系统发送短信。

[5]2008 年四川汶川大地震后，灾区电话无法接通，手机信号中断。救援人员将北斗导航终端带入灾区，及时[6]保持了与外界的通讯联络。

译文 ① BeiDou Navigation Satellite System (BDS), while less advanced than GPS in terms of positioning precision, has new functions of short message communications and position report. With the help of short message communications, users can send messages in the absence of mobile phone signals. For example, after the devastating Wenchuan earthquake in China in 2008, both telephones and mobile phones failed to work. Relief forces, [7]in that case, resorted to BDS and restored local communications in no time.

---

1   successfully 属于多余的副词修饰。"建成"包含了"成功"的意思，英语中语义不用重复。

2   BeiDou Satellite Navigation Experimental System 不是官方译法，官方译法为 BeiDou Navigation Satellite Demonstration System，见译文①。

3   "通信"译为 communications，用复数；单数形式是"交流"的意思。

4   "用户也可以通过该系统发送短信"中的"该系统"应该理解为"该系统的短报通信"功能，而不是整个系统。汉语有时表达不够具体，要结合上下文进行理解。

5   "2008 年四川汶川大地震"是一个例子，对前面"在没有手机信号的地方，用户也可以通过该系统发送短信"进行证明，翻译时增译 For example，前后衔接更加顺畅。另外，英语的举例不会放在段首，而是直接放在被证明对象的后面，所以这两个段落可以合译为一个段落。

6   "及时保持了与外界的通讯联络"应理解为"及时恢复了与外界的通讯联络"。如果将"保持"译为 keep，则译文意思为：之前通讯联络正常，现在依旧保持。而原文的意思是：之前因为地震联络已经断掉，现在恢复了通讯联络。汉语表达有时比较灵活，其真正意义也许与字面意思不一致，要联系上下文进行理解。

7   增译 in that case，前后衔接更加顺畅。

② Though it lags behind America's GPS in positioning ⁸accuracy, BeiDou has two unique functions that GPS lacks—short-message communication and location reporting. In places where there is no mobile phone signal, BeiDou users can use the short-message communication function to send text messages.

After the devastating Wenchuan earthquake ⁹struck in 2008, all phones in the disaster areas stopped working due to the lack of ¹⁰mobile phone signals. BeiDou user terminals were sent to the areas, which was vital for messages to be communicated to the outside world in a timely manner.

该系统的位置报告功能可以帮助交通管理部门掌握行驶车辆的位置，及时疏导交通，缓解交通拥堵 ¹¹ 状况。

译文　① Thanks to the function of position report, traffic departments can track moving vehicles and promptly disperse them to reduce traffic jam.

② The location reporting function can allow transport department to track vehicles in real time, so that the department can better cope with a traffic jam ¹²when it occurs, thus easing the congestion.

虽然北斗导航系统是中国独立发展、自主运行的 ¹³ 卫星导航系统，但这并不影响它与世界上其他卫星导航系统之间的兼容性。用户在同时使用北斗和 GPS 这两种导航系统时，定位和导航效果会更好。

译文　① BDS, independently developed and operated by China, is not incompatible with its international counterparts. A combined use of it and GPS will bring better positioning and navigation.

② ¹⁴Despite the fact that it was developed and run by China independently, BeiDou Satellite Navigation System is compatible with the world's other ¹⁵satellite navigation systems. Users

---

8　此处"精度"应用 precision（强调精确），而不是 accuracy（强调准确）。

9　the devastating Wenchuan earthquake in 2008 已经暗含了 struck（灾难等爆发）之意，故去掉 struck 表达也对，且更简洁。

10　有漏译，"电话（指座机电话）"没有翻出来。

11　"状况"是范畴词，略去不翻。

12　when it occurs 多余，没有实质意义，可省去不译。

13　"卫星导航系统"和前面的"北斗导航系统"存在语意重复，"北斗导航系统"就是"卫星导航系统"，所以"卫星导航系统"略去不翻。

14　用 Though 替换 Despite the fact that，可使译文更简洁。

15　satellite navigation systems 重复太多，可用其他表达灵活替换，比如 counterparts。

would enjoy ¹⁶better positioning and navigation services when ¹⁷BeiDou and GPS are used at the same time.

◆◆◆ 知识点评 ◆◆◆

（1）避开从句

译例 1 **在没有手机信号的地方，用户也可以通过该系统发送短信。**

译文 ① With the help of short message communications, users can send messages in the absence of mobile phone signals.

② In places where there is no mobile phone signal, BeiDou users can use the short-message communication function to send text messages.

分析 "在没有手机信号的地方"可以译为 in the absence of mobile phone signals，译文紧凑且简洁。译文②使用 where 引导的定语从句，语法也对，但不够简洁。

译例 2 **该系统的位置报告功能可以帮助交通管理部门掌握行驶车辆的位置，及时疏导交通，缓解交通拥堵状况。**

译文 ① Thanks to the function of position report, traffic departments can track moving vehicles and promptly disperse them to reduce traffic jam.

② The location reporting function can allow transport department to track vehicles in real time, so that the department can better cope with a traffic jam when it occurs, thus easing the congestion.

分析 如果直译本句，可以译为 "The function of position report helps traffic departments track moving vehicles, so that it can promptly disperse them to reduce traffic jam."。译文①没有直译，而是把"该系统的位置报告功能"作为一个原因状语，这样避免了使用 so that 引导的从句，表达更加简单。译文②有两个从句，so that 引导的结果状语从句和 when 引导的时间状语从句，译文不够简洁。有时在语意不变的前提下，对原文信息进行重组翻译可以使译文更简洁。

译例 3 **用户在同时使用北斗和 GPS 这两种导航系统时，定位和导航效果会更好。**

译文 ① A combined use of it and GPS will bring better positioning and navigation.

② Users would enjoy better positioning and navigation services when BeiDou and GPS are used at the same time.

分析 "同时使用北斗和 GPS 这两种导航系统时"可处理为名词短语 A combined use of...and... 作主语，从而避开使用 when 引导的时间状语从句。是否使用从句要看表达需要，简单信息一般用不上从句，但当原文信息用单词或短语难以表达的时候，可以考虑用从句来表达。

16　"定位和导航效果会更好"可以译为：better services in positioning and navigation，而不是 better positioning and navigation services。

17　BeiDou 不是官方认可的缩写，官方缩写为 BDS。

(2) 使用分隔结构

　　一般情况下，句子中的某些成分应该紧靠在一起，如主语和谓语，谓语和宾语，修饰语与被修饰语等。但有时候，由于各种原因，这些本应紧密连接的句子成分被其他成分隔离，这种语言现象叫作隔离。起分隔作用的有短语（介词短语、分词短语、不定式短语等）、从句、附加成分（插入语、同位语、独立结构）等。

译例 4　**虽然目前北斗导航系统的定位精度与 GPS 还有一定的差距，但它具备了 GPS 所没有的短报通信和位置报告的功能。**

译文　BeiDou Navigation Satellite System (BDS), while less advanced than GPS in terms of positioning precision, has new functions of short message communications and position report.

分析　"但它具备了……"是原文的主句，语义的重心。英译时，主句可以作为"树干"，while 引导的让步状语从句作为分隔结构插在主句的主谓中间。分隔结构在英语中非常普遍，符合英语读者的阅读习惯。阅读中可以多留意英语的分隔结构，灵活运用在自己的译文中。

译例 5　**虽然北斗导航系统是中国独立发展、自主运行的卫星导航系统，但这并不影响它与世界上其他卫星导航系统之间的兼容性。**

译文　BDS, independently developed and operated by China, is not incompatible with its international counterparts.

分析　本译例和译例 4 类似。原文"虽然"引导让步状语从句，后面是主句。英译时，可以先确定主句的主干（BDS is not incompatible），再把从句译文放主句主谓之间。本例中，分隔结构直接对前面主语进行解释说明，有助于语义的连贯。如果把 independently developed and operated by China 放在句首，虽然也符合语法规则，但是读者要读到主句才知道被说明的对象是 BDS。所以，本译例中分隔结构的使用不仅使译文结构紧凑、语意连贯，也便于读者快速捕捉句子重心。

第 7 讲　谚语之翻译

谚语就是对各种生活现象进行综合概括并在群众中广泛流传运用的语言。绝大部分谚语是劳动人民对长期生活经验的总结。汉语谚语与各国文化中的谚语都有这样的特点：比喻生动，寓意深刻；用词精炼，语言简洁；单句讲究韵律，双句讲究对仗，读来朗朗上口，便于记忆流传。如：

- 明枪易躲，暗箭难防。
- 城门失火，殃及池鱼。
- 路遥知马力，日久见人心。
- 聪明一世，糊涂一时。
- 初生牛犊不怕虎。
- 此地无银三百两。
- 三思而后行。
- 玩火者必自焚。

谚语的翻译往往涉及比喻形象的翻译问题，和成语的翻译方法相似，一般也是采用直译、意译和套译三种方法。

第 1 节　直译法

由于大多数谚语采用生动形象的比喻，所以只要不影响译文读者的理解，我们应尽可能使用直译方法，把原文的形象、形式和精神都输入到译文中去，努力减少翻译中的损失。如：

译例 1　路遥知马力，日久见人心。

译文　As a long road tests a horse's strength, so a long task proves a person's heart.

译例 2　初生牛犊不怕虎。

译文　New-born calves make little of tigers.

译例 3　明枪易躲，暗箭难防。

译文　It is easy to dodge a spear in the open, but hard to guard against an arrow shot from hiding.

译例 4　城门失火，殃及池鱼。

译文　A fire on the city gate brings disaster to the fish in the moat.

译例 5　巧妇难为无米之炊。

译文　The cleverest housewife can't cook a meal without rice.

译例 6　留得青山在，不怕没柴烧。

译文　As long as the green hills last, there'll always be wood to burn.

分析　上述谚语中的比喻生动形象，直译后译文读者也能领会其深层意义。如果意译，就无法传达原文中的比喻形象，这是翻译中不应有的损失。例如，如果将译例 1、2 分别意译为 "...time reveals a person's heart." 和 "Young people are fearless."，就无法保留原文的生动和活力。

第 2 节　意译法

由于语言或文化背景上的差异，有些谚语无法直译。这种谚语一般比喻意义较弱，甚至根本没有运用比喻，或者涉及特殊的文化背景。直译会使译文缺乏可读性，导致译文读者无法理解，因此可以采用意译的翻译方法。

译例 1　塞翁失马，焉知非福。

译文　A loss may turn out to be a gain.

译例 2　此地无银三百两。

译文　A guilty person gives himself away by conspicuously protesting his innocence.

译例 3　行行出状元。

译文　Every profession produces its own leading authority.

译例 4　情人眼里出西施。

译文　Beauty lies in lover's eye.

分析　当谚语源自一个典故的时候，如"塞翁失马，焉知非福""此地无银三百两"，直译没法传达原故事内涵，因为读者也许并不了解这个故事。另外，涉及中国文化中一些独特概念或人名的谚语，比如"状元""西施"，也不宜直译。如果直译，译文读者可能会不知所云，因为他们缺乏相关的文化背景。总而言之，若直译可能会导致理解障碍，就需灵活采用意译的方法。

最后再强调一点，意译是对谚语内涵进行解释，而解释方式是非常灵活的，所以没有唯一的译文，只要能传达原文内涵，均可接受。例如："塞翁失马，焉知非福"可以译为"A loss may turn out to be a gain."，也可译为"Behind bad luck comes good luck."。

第 3 节　套译法

有些汉语谚语和英语谚语虽然形象不同，但在意义或内涵上一致。对于这些谚语，我们可以采用套译法，即直接使用英语中已有的对应谚语来表达原文的内涵。如：

译例 1　三思而后行。

译文　Look before you leap.

译例 2　三个臭皮匠，胜过诸葛亮。

译文　Two heads are better than one.

译例 3　失之毫厘，谬以千里。

译文　A miss is as good as a mile.

译例 4　事实胜于雄辩。

译文　Actions speak louder than words.

译例 5　一次被火烧，二次避火苗。

译文　A burnt child dreads the fire.

译例 6　龙生龙，凤生凤。

译文　Like begets like.

译例 7　鹬蚌相争，渔翁得利。

译文　When shepherds quarrel, the wolf has a winning game.

分析　上述中国谚语在英语中均存在对等或基本对等的英语表达，可以选择套译法。这种译文一方面更容易为英语国家读者所理解和接受，另一方面可以给予其亲切感。

总体来说，谚语翻译可以使用三种方法：直译、意译和套译。翻译时，尽量用直译的方法翻译谚语。当直译不能为读者所理解和接受时，可以优先考虑套译，然后再考虑意译。

最后，谚语翻译要注意口语化。谚语是劳动人民对长期生活经验的总结，通俗易懂，语体更接近日常口语。因此，翻译谚语不能文绉绉的，应避免使用学究式语言，尽量使用简单易懂、口语化的表达方式。

真题译·注·评

◆◆◆ 译文对比 ◆◆◆

　　中国每年的总产值，约占世界百分之十，却消耗着世界上百分之四十以上的能源。中国这样一个庞大体，[1] 其一呼一吸，地球是有感觉的。（安徽大学·真题）

译文 ① China makes up 10% of the total output value of the world, but consumes over 40% of the world's energy resources. Every movement and act of such a giant has a great impact on the earth.

② China has 10 percent of the world's [2]gross domestic product, [3]while it consumed more than forty percent of the world's energy resources. If such a giant sneezes, the earth will catch a cold.

　　人类毕竟是自然界的一部分。在整个生态系统中，[4]我们应真正体现出"天人合一"整体观的传统智慧。须知，规律是不可违反的，否则就要受到惩罚。正如恩格斯所说，人类向大自然的每一次索取，都得到了应有的报复。中国谚语也说，[5]"不是不报，时候未到"。我们现在面对的污染，正是对我们以往索取的报应，[6]而其严重与持续程度，亦与索取成正比。

译文 ① Human beings, after all, are part of the nature. We should follow the traditional wisdom "the unity of man and nature" to protect the ecological system. We must know that laws are inviolable，otherwise we will suffer or be punished. As Engels says, "Human beings have got their due revenge for every taking from nature." A Chinese idiom also says, "Punishment will fall on you eventually." The pollution we face now is caused by nothing but our excessive taking from the nature. The seriousness of the pollution and how long it will last are also in proportion to how much we have taken from the nature.

　　1　中国这样一个庞大体，其一呼一吸，地球是有感觉的。这里"一呼一吸"是拟人的修辞手法，如果直译，译文没有可读性。翻译时，可以解释这句话的意思，即中国这样一个大国的一举一动对世界都有着重要影响。因此可以意译为 Every movement and act of such a giant has a great impact on the earth。

　　2　"总产值"的英语是 the total output value，不是 gross domestic product（国内生产总值）。

　　3　while 在这里属于连词误用。while 是对比式转折，用于描述两个对象相反的变化，例如 "The sales of American cars increased while that of Chinese cars decreased."，而原文此句只谈论了 China（中国）这一个对象。

　　4　我们应真正体现出"天人合一"整体观的传统智慧。"真正"没有实质意义，属于多余的副词修饰，故省译；"'天人合一'整体观"中的"整体观"属于范畴词，因为"天人合一"就是把天和人看作一个整体，故可省译"整体观"。

　　5　"不是不报，时候未到"是一句汉语谚语，由于其未涉及比喻形象，比喻意义较弱，故翻译时可采用意译的方法，用简单的语言解释它的意思，即 "Punishment will fall on you eventually（报应早晚会到来）."。

　　6　"而其严重与持续程度"完整的理解是"污染的严重程度与持续时间"。原文中的"持续程度"表达并不好，这是原文的问题。原文中的"持续程度"指的就是持续时间，翻译时应学会理解变通。

② After all, human beings are a part of nature. We should follow the rule—[7] "people and nature live in harmony"—[8]the traditional Chinese wisdom of overall view. We must know that, if we are against natural rules, we will be punished by nature. [9]Just as the Engels' saying goes, people will get what they deserve with the devastation they did to the nature. There's another Chinese old saying, "Punishment will fall on you eventually." Our overexploitation of nature results in the pollution that we are facing now. [10]The more natural resources we overexploited, the more pollution we made.

生产不是为了使生活更美好吗？如果不是，又是为了什么？诚如《圣经》所[11]讲，[12]赚得了全世界，而毁掉了自己，又有什么意义？所以，对于"发展是硬道理"要有[13]更全面、科学的理解。简言之，只有[14]良性、平衡、有益于人们生活的发展才是硬道理。

译文 ① Isn't production meant to increase our well-being? If not, then for what? As is warned in the Bible, what can we get if we win the world but destroy ourselves? Therefore, we should have a thorough and more scientific understanding of the principle "development is the top priority". Put simply, only healthy, well-balanced and life-benefiting development is the top priority.

② Did we improve our producing capabilities in order to make the life more beautiful? If not, then what's the purpose of the improvement? Bible says, it is meaningless if you earn everything [15]by means of destroying yourselves. Therefore, we need to develop a more comprehensive and scientific understanding on the policy of "development is the top priority". To make it simple, the [16]benign, balanced, and beneficial development is the only priority.

7　people and nature live in harmony 是错误表达，因为 nature 不能作 live 的主语，可以改为 "people live in harmony with nature"。

8　the traditional Chinese wisdom of overall view。这里的"整体观"属于"天人合一"的范畴词，故 overall view 多余。

9　这样的表达偏文学文体，而这篇文章属于时政类文体。时政类文章讲究表达简洁，因此可以将其简化为：As Engels says。

10　这里明显没有理解透原文的意思，也漏译了"持续程度"。

11　根据下文，这里的"讲"应该理解为"警告"。

12　"赚得了全世界，而毁掉了自己"可以看作一个条件状语从句，而且应该放在句尾，否则头重脚轻。

13　"更全面、科学的理解"不能译为：a more thorough and scientific understanding，因为 thorough 没有比较级和最高级，译为 a thorough and more scientific understanding 即可。译文 2 将"更全面"译为了 more comprehensive，用词不准确，因为原文"更全面的理解"指的是更为深入的理解，comprehensive 的内涵是"包含各个方面"，强调的是范围广泛，不符合原文内涵；thorough 强调的是深入思考或调查，符合原文内涵。

14　"良性"可以转化为"健康"，译为 healthy。

15　by means of 是有意识地通过某个方式达到一个目的。这个译文扭曲了原文的逻辑，并不是说通过毁灭自己的方式获得全世界，而是说获得了全世界，代价却是毁灭了自己。

16　benign 是医学上的一个概念，意为"（肿瘤）良性的"，指的是不会给生命带来威胁的意思。本文中的"良性"是指发展"健康"的意思。汉英翻译需要注意的一点是，不能意思一样就硬套，翻译时需要考虑词的内涵、适用领域和搭配。

◆◆◆ 知识点评 ◆◆◆

（1）避开不存在的英语表达

译例 1　正如恩格斯所说，人类向大自然的每一次索取，都得到了应有的报复。

译文　Just as the Engels' saying goes, people will get what they deserve <u>with the devastation they did to the nature</u>.

译例 2　生产不是为了使生活更美好吗？

译文　Did we <u>improve our producing capabilities</u> in order to make the life more beautiful?

分析　以上画横线处都是英语中不存在的表达和搭配。译例 1 中，do devastation to 这样的搭配并不存在，我们学过 do damage to，但不能想当然地以为也存在 do devastation to 这样的表达，我们可以说 cause devastation；译例 2 中，"生产能力"的英语表达为（production）capacity 或 productive power，没有 producing capability 这样的表达。汉英翻译时，不能随意编造表达，应尽可能用简单、熟悉、有把握的表达方式。

（2）注意英语时态

汉语动词没有时态的变化，但英语动词会根据动词发生的时间有不同的时态。时态错误也是学生译文中常见的问题，具体表现在时态误用和时态不一致。以下译例的译文②中皆存在时态误用的问题。

译例 3　**中国每年的总产值，约占世界百分之十，却消耗着世界上百分之四十以上的能源。**

译文　① China makes up 10% of the total output value of the world, but <u>consumes</u> over 40% of the world's energy resources.

② China has 10 percent of the world's gross domestic product, while it <u>consumed</u> more than forty percent of the world's energy resources.

分析　英语中，对客观存在进行说明介绍用一般现在时。该句是对中国每年的总产值和能源使用情况（客观存在）的说明，要用一般现在时。译文②中，后半句用过去时是时态误用。

译例 4　**正如恩格斯所说，人类向大自然的每一次索取，都得到了应有的报复。**

译文　① As Engels says, "Human beings <u>have got their due revenge</u> for every taking from nature."

② Just as the Engels' saying goes, people <u>will get what they deserve</u> with the devastation they did to the nature.

分析　"都得到了应有的报复"表明这个动作已经发生，应用现在完成时。译文②用一般将来时，属时态误用。

第 8 讲 修辞格之翻译

汉语和英语中都存在大量的修辞格，比如：比喻、夸张、拟人、排比、反语等。这些修辞格在描述情景、烘托人物、发展情节、展现风格等方面起着不可或缺的作用。对汉语修辞格的翻译，主要用到直译和意译两种方法。

第 1 节　直译法

修辞格翻译优先考虑直译法，因为直译可以保留原文的形象，使译文同样生动形象。当直译能够被读者理解和接受的时候，就采用直译法。

译例 1 鲜花向着每一位来宾展开了笑容。

译文 The flowers smile at every visitor.

分析 该译例运用了拟人修辞。所谓拟人修辞就是给物赋予人才有的动作或情感。"笑"是人特有的表情，而在本句中却用来指物，鲜花的美丽中融入人的微笑，使气氛显得更加亲切和热烈。直译也完全能为读者所接受。

译例 2 他的口才可以把石头说得动起来。

译文 His eloquence would have moved a stone to action.

分析 该译例运用了夸张修辞，将"他的口才"夸张描述为"可以把石头说得动起来"，用以烘托其口才好。英语译文采用了直译的翻译方法，保留了原文形象"石头（stone）"，不仅不影响读者对原文的理解，而且语言生动形象。

译例 3 他父亲将这对伴侣的新生活比作在漫长而不知终点的轨道上奔驰着的一列火车，"你们的前程可能是蜿蜒曲折的，也许还有阴暗的隧道"，他告诫他们说，"但是我们预祝你们旅途平安。"

译文 His father compared the coupe's new life together to a railroad train on a long, unknown track. "There may be curves and dark tunnels ahead," he told them, "but we wish you a safe journey."

分析 该译例多处运用了隐喻修辞，例如将"这对伴侣的新生活"比作"在漫长而不知终点的轨道上奔驰着的一列火车"以及将"这对伴侣的新生活中未来可能面临的挫折"比作"阴暗的隧道"，汉英翻译时都进行了直译，完整地保留了原文的形象。

译例 4 这位老人含辛茹苦了一辈子，现在安息了。

译文 The old man lay taking his rest after a life of bitter hardship.

分析 汉语和英语中都存在大量委婉说法，这些委婉语往往不能从字面去理解。但是，由于汉、英语中对于一些话题共同的隐晦和委婉表达需要，还是能在两种语言中找到很多契合的说法。一旦情感意义和语体意义比较对等，往往可以直译。该译例中 take one's rest 是"去世"的委婉语，直译读者也完全能够理解原文想要表达的委婉含义。

第 2 节 意译法

有些汉语修辞格的形象，英语国家读者并不熟悉，直译往往会让其感到困惑或难以接受。这个时候，可以采用意译的手段，解释原文的意思。当形式和意义发生冲突的时候，优先传达意义，而不是原文的形式。例如：

译例 1 他前程似锦。

译文 He has a bright future.

分析 译例 1 中，"前程似锦"运用了比喻修辞。"锦"是一种美丽的纺织品，起源于中国，常用于象征美好的事物。英语国家读者可能并不了解这种纺织品以及其象征意义。如果直译，译文对英语国家读者而言没有可读性，因此可以取其意，译为 have a bright future。

译例 2 他们两人经历了婚姻中的低潮和风雨。

译文 They have been through some difficult times in their marriage.

分析 "低潮和风雨"是汉语中特有的比喻"困难"的形象，这里理解为艰难时刻，如果直译，读者很难将它们和婚姻产生语义上的关联，因此翻译时可以采取意译的翻译方法，将其译为 some difficult times。

译例 3 社会保障则是维护社会稳定的重要防线。

译文 Social security is essential for social stability.

分析 "防线"是和战争相关的概念，若直译为 line of defense，语义勉强可以理解，但在这个语境中译文不够自然贴切，也不地道。"重要防线"表达的就是非常重要的意思，翻译时取其意，译为 essential 即可。

译例 4 法律上的平等对他们而言不再是无实际意义的镜中之花、水中之月。

译文 Equality under the law is no longer a mere dream for them.

分析 "镜中之花、水中之月"内涵一致，皆是汉语中独特的比喻"虚空以及不切实际的梦"的形象，英语中没有这种比喻形象，直译的话，译文不仅不好理解，而且表达重复啰嗦。因此，将"镜中之花、水中之月"意译为 a mere dream。

译例 5 在建立多极化的过程中可以寻找到更多的共同语言。

译文 Find more common ground in building a multi-polar world.

分析 "共同语言"是一个比喻的说法，其实是"共同立场"或"共同利益"的意思，译为 common ground 即可。且多极化的一个特点就是各国之间共同利益不断增多。如果直译为 common language，在国家间找共同语言，读者可能会困惑：这与建立多极化有何关联？

由此可见，修辞格是直译还是意译取决于译文的可读性。如果译文读者可以理解原文形象及背后传达的意义，就直译；如果字面意思或原文形象让译文读者感到陌生，不易理解，就意译。

真题译·注·评

◆◆◆ **译文对比** ◆◆◆

¹ 在亚洲各国政府和人民的共同努力下，亚洲的发展正呈现出前所未有的良好态势，突出表现在：² 亚洲巨大的市场潜能逐步得到开发，亚洲各国和地区经济结构调整的成效显著，产业 ³ 优化升级继续加快，经济持续快速发展，亚洲已成为全球经济最具活力的地区之一。（中南大学·真题）

译文 ① Thanks to the joint efforts of all Asian governments and people, Asia is in the midst of unprecedented sound development, marked by the unleashing of huge market potential, effective economic restructuring, accelerating industrial upgrading, and rapid and sustained economic growth. All of these made Asia one of the most dynamic regions in the world.

② Thanks to the joint efforts of the governments and people ⁴ of Asian countries, Asia has witnessed an unprecedented sound momentum of development, marked by the unleashing of huge market potential, effective economic restructuring ⁵ in various countries and areas, accelerating industrial upgrading, and fast and sustained economic growth. This has made Asia one of the most dynamic regions in the world.

⁶ 亚洲和平、稳定、合作的整体氛围促进了亚洲区域合作进程的快速发展。一个平等、多元、开放、互利的地区新局面正在 ⁷ 逐步形成。这些积极而重大的变化，既为推动亚洲区域合作提供

1　"在亚洲各国政府和人民的共同努力下"可以看作一个原因状语，用 Thanks to 引导。thanks to 是一个褒义的表达方式，传达出了原文褒义的感情色彩。如果用 because of，则体现不出原文褒义的感情色彩。

2　亚洲巨大的市场潜能逐步得到开发，亚洲各国和地区经济结构调整的成效显著，产业优化升级继续加快。这个句子存在多处重复表达："亚洲巨大的市场潜能逐步得到开发"中的"亚洲"多余，因为这段文字讲的对象就是亚洲，上下文已经很明确，不需要重复翻译；"亚洲各国和地区经济结构调整成效显著"中的"亚洲各国和地区"指的就是"亚洲"，也是语境暗含的意思，可以省译。因此，译文可以简化为"...the unleashing of huge market potential, effective economic restructuring..."。如果逐字逐句翻译，译文会很啰嗦、冗长，不符合英语的表达习惯。

3　"优化升级"语意重复，翻"升级"即可，因为"升级"包含了"优化"的意思。

4　the joint efforts of the governments and people of Asian countries，最好用 Asian 作前置定语，放到 governments and people 前面，参考译文①，这样表达更简练、结构更紧凑。此外，英语不喜欢连续出现两个介词 of。

5　in various countries and areas 多余，删去，省译理由见脚注 2。

6　亚洲和平、稳定、合作的整体氛围促进了亚洲区域合作进程的快速发展。这个句子中的"氛围"没有实质含义，可以省译，意义没有损失；"促进了亚洲区域合作进程的快速发展"可以简化为"加快亚洲区域合作"，意义没有损失。时政类文体的汉英翻译要注意抓"实"去"虚"（后者指可有可无的东西），根据简化后的汉语翻译，对应生成一篇地道的、言简意赅的英语译文。

7　"逐步形成"中的"逐步"是多余的副词修饰，没有实质意义，故可省译。

了有利条件，也为亚洲各国和地区的发展带来了历史性机遇。⁸ 只要我们继续相互尊重、平等对待，把握发展的机会，把握住自己的命运，就一定能够促进亚洲的发展与振兴，达致互利共赢的目标。

译文 ① The overall peace, stability and cooperation have accelerated the regional development in Asia. A new type of regional cooperation based on equality, diversity, opening up and mutual benefits is taking shape. These major positive changes have provided favorable conditions for regional cooperation and good opportunities for Asian development as well. We should continue to respect and treat each other as equals, seize the opportunities and hold destiny in our own hands. As long as we can do these, we will certainly get mutual benefits and win-win progress and promote Asian development and rejuvenation.

② The overall peace, stability and development in Asia have led to fast progress in the regional cooperation [9]process. A new type of regional cooperation based on equality, diversity, openness and mutual benefits is taking shape. These positive and major developments have brought about both favorable conditions for regional cooperation and historical opportunities for [10]the development of Asia. We should respect and treat each other as equals, seize the opportunities of development and hold our destiny in our own hands. As we do this, we will certainly achieve mutual benefit and win-win progress and promote development and rejuvenation of Asia.

◆◆◆ 知识点评 ◆◆◆

（1）句尾重心

英语句子通常把重要的信息放在尾部，使它得到必要的强调。如：

例 1 拓 Einstein is a fair violist, a great mathematician, and a deeply philosophical man.

分析 上例是说，爱因斯坦有三重身份：他既是伟大的数学家，又是个精深哲理的哲学家，同时还是个业余小提琴手。爱因斯坦的主要成就体现在物理领域和哲学领域，这里并未提及物理学家的身份，所以哲学家的身份较另外两个身份而言，应该是最重要的。这三重身份当中，哲学家最重要，数学家次之，业余小提琴又次之。所以，依据英语句尾重心的特点，三重身份按 a fair violist, a great mathematician, and a deeply philosophical man 这样的顺序排列。

8　只要我们继续相互尊重、平等对待，把握发展的机会，把握住自己的命运，就一定能够促进亚洲的发展与振兴，达致互利共赢的目标。如果直译，条件状语从句会很长，而现代英语提倡简明英语，并不喜欢句子太长。因此，可以拆开翻译，汉语转化为：我们应该继续相互尊重、平等对待，把握发展的机会，把握住自己的命运。只要可以做到这些，就一定能够促进亚洲的发展与振兴，达致互利共赢的目标。

9　"亚洲区域合作进程"中的"进程"为范畴词，可以省译，process 多余。

10　将 the development of Asia 改为 Asian development，译文更简洁，参考译文①。

例 2　This law should meet with your approval because it is simple, because it is enforceable and because it is just.

分析　上例是关于一条法律，到底是"立法公正"重要呢？还是"切实可行"、"简单明了"重要呢？当然，一条法律首先要求"公正"，"可行"次之，"明了"又次之，所以可以按句中的次序安排。

汉英翻译时，对一些并列结构，可以把最重要的信息放在译文句尾。

译例 1　**只要我们继续相互尊重、平等对待，把握发展的机会，把握住自己的命运，就一定能够促进亚洲的发展与振兴，达致互利共赢的目标。**

译文　We should continue to respect and treat each other as equals, seize the opportunities and hold destiny in our own hands. As long as we can do these, we will certainly get mutual benefits and win–win progress and promote Asian development and rejuvenation.

分析　原文顺序是"促进亚洲的发展与振兴，达致互利共赢的目标"，前者明显比后者更加重要，所以译文对表达顺序进行了调整，将"促进亚洲的发展与振兴"置于句尾翻译。

（2）渐降法

渐降法是一种修辞手段，指故意打破由次要到重要的顺序，把不太重要的信息放在最后、最重要的位置上，目的是达到幽默、讽刺的修辞效果或通过反差给读者留下深刻印象。

例 3　For God, for America, and for Yale.（耶鲁大学校训）

分析　同"上帝（God）"和"国家（America）"相比，"一所学校（Yale）"的重要性当然小得多，顺序上可算是一种渐降。但其却被放在句尾的重心位置上，正是因为这种反差，反而给人留下格外深刻的印象，使学生认识到要从耶鲁做起、从我做起。

例 4　He owes his success to hard work, perseverance, and his father-in law.

分析　一个人事业的成功，最重要因素本应为"埋头苦干（hard work）"和"坚韧不拔（perseverance）"。可是译文却把"老丈人（father-in law）"这一裙带关系放在最后、最重要的位置上，这明显是为了讽刺。

汉英翻译时，对于汉语原文出现渐降法修辞的句子，英语译文的并列顺序应和原文保持一致，从而达到相同的修辞效果。

译例 2　**经过长时间的攀登，终于到达顶峰。我们欣赏着美丽的风景，呼吸着新鲜的空气，感受着脚底的疼痛。**

译文　The long climb to the summit rewarded us with a spectacular view, invigorating air, and sore feet.

分析　一群人经过努力攀登，终于到了山顶，本应有"一览众山小"的广阔胸襟，却把"脚底的疼痛"放在最后最重要的位置，这显然是故意打趣，表示幽默。译文和原文顺序保持一致，同样达到了幽默的效果。

篇章翻译

第 9 讲　文学翻译

文学是通过语言文字来表达思想和情感的艺术形式，是人类文化的重要组成部分。和其他作品相比，文学作品具有以下四个特点：

一、文学作品的载体是语言文字，既需要表现出语言的艺术美感，又需要传达出作者所要表达的思想情感；

二、文学作品具有高度的艺术性，不仅仅是一种信息传递的工具，更是一种审美的享受；

三、文学作品是作者个性的反映，在表现形式、内容和风格等方面具有独特性；

四、文学作品是时代文化的产物，反映了时代的思想、观念和价值观。

文学作品有不同的分类标准。按体裁来分，文学大致可分为四类：散文、戏剧、诗歌和小说。文学翻译是翻译硕士考试的重要考试题型，也是难度较大的一种题型。历年各高校考查散文翻译较多，其他体裁很少涉及，所以本讲主要分析散文作品的翻译。

第 1 节　散文特点

散文是与戏剧、诗歌、小说并列的文学体裁，主要包括记叙散文、抒情散文和哲理散文。记叙散文指以写人、记事为主的散文，通过描写人物或叙述事情来表达作者的思想感情；抒情散文注重抒发作者对现实生活的感受；哲理散文重在阐述人生哲理、智慧和感悟，通常具有深刻的思考和独到的见解，帮助读者理解生活的意义和价值，启迪人们的心灵。散文主要特点包括：

1.1　形散神聚

所谓"形散"，含义有三：一是取材广泛，二是结构多变，三是表达自由。所谓"神聚"，则指主题集中。散文无论篇幅长短，无论其外在的"形"如何散乱，其内在的"神"总是明确而集中的。以朱自清的《背影》为例。这篇散文叙述了"父亲与儿子一起回家奔丧；父亲因担心儿子亲自送儿子去火车站；因儿子行李太多雇人帮拿行李；父亲在火车上为儿子仔细挑选座位；父亲爬过月台给儿子买橘子"等事件。文中的事件看似零散，但仔细分析就会发现其间的联系，所有的事都是围绕着父亲对儿子的爱而安排的。父亲的爱以及儿子对父亲的思念，便是这篇文章的"神"，即主题。

1.2　意境创造

意境创造指通过语言的艺术手段，营造出一种特定的情景或氛围。文学作品中的意境可以深入读者心灵，引发读者情感共鸣。例如：老舍作品《济南的冬天》从不同的角度描绘了济南冬天独有的美，语言生动形象，在读者脑海中勾画出一幅济南的冬景图：温暖宁静、天空蔚蓝、河水清澈、水藻碧绿、小山环绕等。品读起来，使人产生"身临其境"之感。

1.3　语言优美

　　散文素有"美文"之称，其语言通常凝练、生动、优美，充满诗情画意。作者往往运用各种修辞手法，如比喻、拟人、排比等，使散文的语言更加富有表现力和感染力。此外，散文的语言优美还体现在韵律美，作者通过抑扬顿挫、富有情感的音韵节奏，使散文读起来或如流水汩汩或如锣鼓铿锵。

　　了解散文的上述特点有助于翻译的理解和表达。散文翻译首先要对原文有透彻的理解，包括原文主题、语言特征、思想情感、内容结构等。其次，在表达的时候，要注意意境、节奏及美感再现等，而不仅仅是内容保持一致。

第 2 节　散文翻译标准

2.1　信之译文

　　"信"指译文内容忠实原文、意义不悖原文，是翻译最基本也是最重要的原则之一。散文虽多是抒发情感，与科技翻译、时政翻译等文体相比客观性弱一些，但其翻译也要遵守这一原则。汉语散文英译时，首先要理解透原文，用恰当的语言忠实传达原文内容。在理解的过程中，有时不仅要参考原文语境以及原文的社会文化背景，还要运用逻辑推理，做到理解无误。

译例 1　学院请来一位洋教师，长得挺怪，红脸，金发，连鬓大胡须，有几根胡子一直逾过面颊，挨近鼻子。（冯骥才《西式幽默》）

译文　Our institute employed an English teacher. He looked very strange—red-faced, golden-haired with a thick growth of whiskers that reached all the way to the nose. （Denis C. Mair 译）

分析　原文是对洋教师外表的描述。红脸、金发、连鬓大胡须等特征说明他的外表不同于国人普遍长相，所以此处的"怪"是指洋教师外表不寻常。因此，"长得挺怪"可以译为 unusual。若直译为 very strange，译文则不够忠实，因为 strange 带有贬义，有"奇怪到使人感到紧张或害怕"之义，不符合原文的语境。由此可见，散文翻译应结合语境分析，对原文用词的"度"有一个准确的把握，在翻译时精确选词，从而实现译文的忠实。

译例 2　请闭上眼睛想：一个老城，有山有水，全在天底下晒着阳光，暖和安适地睡着，只等春风来把它们唤醒，这是不是个理想的境界？（老舍《济南的冬天》）

译文　Close your eyes and just picture: an old town in the midst of hills and water is sleeping cozily in the sunshine and would not wake up until the call of a spring breeze. Is it a utopia?

分析　作者在脑海中勾画出一幅关于济南的想象图。如果把"有山有水"中的"山水"直译为 hills and water，译文内容传达则不够准确。因为每个城市都有 water，并不稀奇。且 water 几乎是人每日必备摄入，对于长久干旱之地，将 water 视为理想可以理解。但济南并非久旱之地，结合济南的地理环境可知，济南有很多著名的湖泊，如大明湖、历阳湖等，这是区别于中国大多城市的一个特点。因此，为忠实传达原文内涵，这里的"水"应理解为"湖泊"，译为 lakes。此外，hills 与 lakes 均为可数名词复数，二者并列，较 hills and water 而言，形式上也更忠实于原文。

译例 3　儿时的乡村，是可以夜不闭户的。（北京外国语大学·真题）

译文　When I was a child, the villagers could leave the doors open at night without worrying about thefts.

分析　"夜不闭户"意指夜间睡觉不用关门、不怕小偷来侵犯，形容社会治安良好。上述译文虽字面意思忠实于原文，但"leave the doors open..."，不符合语境逻辑以及生活常识。英语国家读者看到此译文，或许会心生困惑：难道冬天也开门睡觉？此外，根据生活常识可知，关门睡觉素来是人们的生活习惯。这里的"夜不闭户"理解为"晚上不用锁门"更符合语境逻辑,译为 leave the doors unlocked at night without worrying about thefts,这样译文既符合现实生活中人们的生活习惯,又表达出了不怕小偷窃取东西的放心。译文传递意义准确,不悖原文。

2.2 达之译文

"达"指译文要通顺晓畅。散文英译应在准确理解原文、忠实传达原文的基础上,用符合目的语表达习惯的语言传达原文旨意。在这一过程中,为了使译文通顺,在忠实原文意义的前提下,可以不拘泥于原文形式,进行适当的增译或减译,也可以对原文信息进行重组。

译例 4 我忐忑不安、心慌意乱。我想对他们说停车停车我要下去,可话到嘴边却张不开口。毕竟,他们还没把你怎么着;再揉眼看看窗外,行车的路线也对头啊。看来,今儿我只好豁出去,听天由命了! (张抗抗《恐惧的平衡》)

译文 I was on pins and needles. I wanted to stop the car and get out, but couldn't bring myself to say so. After all they haven't done anything to me. I looked out of the window. Yes, we were travelling in the right direction. I will just have to risk it, I thought to myself. (朱虹 译)

分析 原文主语不断变换,从"我"转到"他们",再转到"行车的路线",最后再回归到"我",读起来错综变化,但其主题明确,呈现出散文典型的"形散神聚"特点。在英语中,叙述的视角(句子主语)应尽量保持一致,不要频繁变动,否则不符合英语的表达习惯。故翻译时,让人称"我(I)"作主语,基本贯穿始终(we 属于半重复,因为"I"也是其中的一个)。此外,Yes 的增译也很到位,不仅使前后内容衔接更加顺畅,而且形象地展现了主人公当时的心理状态。

译例 5 大概是因为正在下午的缘故吧,这回说是酒楼,却毫无酒楼气,我已经喝下三杯酒去了,而我以外还是四张空板桌。(鲁迅《在酒楼上》)

译文 Perhaps because it was only the afternoon, no aroma of wine permeated the shop. Even after I had downed the third cup, the upstairs was still empty, save for myself and four unoccupied tables. (William A. Lyell 译)

分析 原文"一逗到底",却可以第三个分句结束为节点,分为两层意思。第二层在意思上是第一层的递进。因此,翻译时,增译 Even after,不仅有助于第二句译文主从句的衔接,而且和前文的递进关系也得到了体现。增译后的译文不仅非常通顺,而且逻辑关系清晰,很好地传达了原文的内在关系。如果不增译,译文第一句和第二句的衔接便会有点生硬。

译例 6 官复原职的 N 省建材局杨局长和李秘书,走在蒿草丛生、芦荻疏落的湖边。"烟中列岫青无数,雁背夕阳红欲暮。"西风,秋水,雁阵,衔着落日的远山,交融在一起,更增添打猎者的无限兴致。(徐光兴《枪口》)

译文 Mr. Yang, the reinstated head of the Bureau of Building Material of N Province, and his secretary Mr. Li were walking through the tall grass and sparse reeds along the lakeside. The crisp west wind, the lucid autumn waters, the V's of wild geese and the glowing mountains at sunset were exactly what was depicted by an ancient poem: "Mountain peaks rise above the distant blue; The southbound geese glow in the sunset red." The scene couldn't hut heighten one's hunting spirit.（张光前 译）

分析 "西风，秋水，雁阵，衔着落日的远山"是故事发生时的场景，由此想到一句诗词"烟中列岫青无数，雁背夕阳红欲暮"。该诗词意境和故事场景非常相似，表现了故事主人公当时的心境。原文以诗词开头，再描述实景，而英语一般先描述实景，再发表评论。故翻译时，作者在理解原文的基础上，对信息进行了一定的重组。先翻译具体实景"西风，秋水，雁阵，衔着落日的远山"（The crisp west wind, the lucid autumn waters, the V's of wild geese and the glowing mountains at sunset），再进行评论。由于二者意境相似，译者把两部分合译，诗歌内容处理成评价部分（...were exactly what was depicted by an ancient poem: "Mountain peaks rise above the distant blue; The southbound geese glow in the sunset red."）。经过这番处理，整个译文浑然天成，读起来非常通顺，可谓"达"。

2.3 雅之译文

散文翻译的"雅"体现在多个层面，如用词雅、修辞雅、音韵雅。一篇"雅"的译文可以实现内容、形式和意境的完美统一，使译文具有原文同等的艺术感染力，给读者带来相同的情感体验，或在读者脑海中产生相同的意象。

译例 7 北京的冬季，地上还有积雪，灰黑色的秃树枝丫杈于晴朗的天空中，而远处有一二风筝浮动，在我是一种惊异和悲哀。（鲁迅《风筝》）

译文 When, in late winter in Beijing, there was still snow on the ground and, up in the air, an entanglement of dark-gray bare branches against a sunny sky, a couple of kites were already fluttering up and down in the distance — a sight that filled me with amazement and forlornness.

（刘士聪 译）

分析 原文通过积雪、秃树枝丫和风筝描绘了一幅北京残冬的画面，给人一种苍凉和悲伤的感觉。作者触景生情，想起童年往事，"惊异和悲哀"之情油然而生。翻译时，译者用 late winter、an entanglement of dark-gray bare branches 营造出一种冬日雪后树木萧瑟的情景，用词贴切；原文"灰黑色的秃树枝丫杈于晴朗的天空中"运用了对比修辞，翻译时，用 against 一词凸显"萧瑟之景"与"晴朗天空"这一鲜明对比。接着译文顺承而下，用 a couple of kites were already fluttering up and down in the distance 指出那晴朗天空中令"我"惊异的画面——远处有一二风筝浮动。这一画面引出下文作者讲述令其感到悲哀的童年往事。译文通过精准用词和重现修辞，勾勒出一个与原文相同的画面，再现了原文情景交融的意境，使读者有身临其境之感。

译例 8 曲曲折折的荷塘上面，弥望的是田田的叶子。叶子出水很高，像亭亭的舞女的裙。层层的叶子中间，零星地点缀着些白花……（朱自清《荷塘月色》）

译文 All over this winding stretch of water what meets the eyes is a silken field of leaves, reaching above the surface, like the skirts of dancing girls in all their grace. Here and there, layers of leaves are dotted with white lotus blossoms.（朱纯深 译）

分析　原文描绘了月下荷塘的美景，语言清新自然，景物描写细腻传神，具有强烈的画面感。最先映入眼帘的是满塘荷叶，"亭亭"一词表现了荷叶的风姿秀丽，"舞女裙"的比喻，恰到好处地展现了荷叶临风摇曳的姿态。此外，叠词"曲曲折折""田田""亭亭"和"层层"的使用，韵律鲜明，产生了一种悦耳动听的节奏感。翻译时，在再现原文景物形象的同时，利用英语中的头韵（winding、water、what；layers、leaves）修辞再现了原文的音韵美。总体来说，上述译文对景物的描绘细致入微、形象生动，不仅语言优美，意境也同样优美。

译例 9　对于一个在北平住惯的人，像我，冬天要是不刮大风，便是奇迹；济南的冬天是没有风声的。对于一个刚由伦敦回来的人，像我，冬天要能看得见日光，便是怪事；济南的冬天是响晴的。（老舍《济南的冬天》）

译文　For someone like me who is used to living in Beijing, a winter without any wind is a bit of miracle. Well, one never hears any whistling winter winds in Jinan. For someone like me who has just returned from London, sunshine in the winter seems quite unusual. Well, Jinan has bright sunny winter weather.（施晓菁 译）

分析　原文包含两个平行结构：对于……像我……便是……济南的冬天是……。平行结构通过结构的对称产生一种独特的韵律或节奏，不仅可以表达丰富的情感，而且给读者以美的感受，给他们留下更深刻的印象。翻译时，为体现原文的节奏美，译文同样运用了平行结构，以期对读者产生相同或类似的效果。此外，"Well"的增译非常到位，不仅有助于和前句的衔接以及表达的通顺，该词的口语色彩也非常符合原文的语域。总的来说，译文再现了原文的修辞美和语体美。

第 3 节　散文翻译要点

3.1　把握原文风格

风格是作者在文学作品中表现出来的创作个性。不同的作者和作品往往有着不同的语言风格，比如：正式与非正式、简洁与繁复、朴实与华丽等。风格的传递是散文翻译的一大难点。翻译的时候，首先要把握原文的风格，再用恰当的语言把原文风格再现出来。

译例 1　A：您家掌柜的卖过血吗？

B：（身份为农村妇女）<u>没有。我不让他卖。对身体不好。家里全指望他干活。女的没有男的干活出力大。那时候孩子都小，两人不能都出去。</u>

译文　①No. I don't want him to because it may do harm to his health. The children and I have to rely on him for our living. It's different for me since I'm unable to contribute as much as my husband in terms of working in the fields. And our children were very young at that time, so only one of us may sell blood for money and the other must stay healthy to take care of the children.

②No. I won't let him. It's bad for the health. The whole family counts on him to work. Women aren't as strong as men, and the kids were still young anyway so one of us had to stay home.

分析　首先，这是一个采访，语言风格偏口语性质；其次，还要考虑讲话者是一个农村妇女身份。一般而言，农村妇女所受教育不多，不大可能以译文①的方式说话。口语不会像书面语一样，句子那么长，而且还运用大量连词以体现句间逻辑关系。英语口语往往用词和句式简单，甚至不需要完整的句子，亦或句子表达不符合语法规范。由于对话双方都很熟悉谈话的背景，逻辑关系往往暗含在语境中，并不需要那么多连词。译文①虽然传达了原文意思，但读起来感觉文绉绉的，没有农村妇女讲话的那种味道。而译文②不仅传达了原文意思，风格也和原文基本一致，表现出了农村妇女讲话的特点。

译例 2　我幼年读过书，虽然不多，可是足够读七侠五义与三国志演义什么的。我记得好几段聊斋，到如今还能说得很齐全动听，不但听的人都夸奖我的记性好，连我自己也觉得应该高兴。可是，我并念不懂聊斋的原文，那太深了；我所记得的几段，都是由小报上的"评讲聊斋"念来的——把原文变成白话，又添上些逗哏打趣，实在有个意思！

（老舍《我这一辈子》）

译文　①I had some schooling when I was young. Though it wasn't much, it was enough education for me to read such novels as *The Seven Heroes and Five Gallants* and *Three Kingdoms*. I know quite a few stories from *Strange Tales from Make-Do Studio* too, and I can retell them vividly even now. People admired me for such a wonderful memory, and I also felt proud of that gift. But I wasn't able to read the books in the original, because classical language was too abstruse. The stories I learned were from the literature columns in newspapers. They were rewritten in plain language and spiced with humour. Those stories were fascinating.

② I studied a bit when I was a boy. Not much, mind you, but enough to read *The Seven Knights and Five Heroes* and *Three Kingdoms* and things like that. I know quite a lot of stories in *Liao Zhai*, by heart—I could tell you them with all the details if you liked. They make good listening. Not that I can read the originals—that classical language is too hard for me. The bits I know I learned from those "Liao Zhai Stories Retold" columns in the papers. They are terrific. They turn the classical stuff into ordinary Chinese, and put jokes in too.

（W. J. F. Jenner 译）

分析　原文叙述就好像作者在和读者对话一样，语体偏口语体。两个译文都做到了忠实、通顺，但译文②口语色彩更加明显，更贴近原文风格。从选词角度来看，译文②中的 a bit、The bits、make good listening、terrific、stuff 以及 put 都是口语化的表达，表达风格贴近原文。从句子角度来看，译文②句式结构更简单、更短，而且还有 "Not much, mind you, but enough to read *The Seven Knights and Five Heroes* and *Three Kingdoms* and things like that." 这样的不完整结构，这些都是口语体的特征。总的来说，译文②更好地再现了原文的风格。

3.2　注意文化差异

翻译不仅仅是语言之间的转换，还要考虑到译文在目的语文化中能否被理解和接受。当文化差异较大，影响译文理解的时候，译者可以通过解释、增译或淡化处理的方式灵活处理文化差异。

译例 3　除了我这间房，大院里还有二十多间房呢。一共住着多少家子，谁说得清？住两间房的就不多，又搭上今儿个搬来，明儿又搬走。我没那么好的记性。大家见面，招呼声"吃了吗？"透着和气。（老舍《柳家大院》）

译文　Besides the room we occupy there are twenty more rooms in the same compound. How many families live there, only God knows. Those who occupy two rooms are very few. Besides, they are always on the go (moving in today and moving out tomorrow). I have not got such a good memory as to remember all that. When people meet, they pass the time of the day with each other, just to show their good neighborly feelings. （张谷若 译）

分析　"吃了吗？"是一种独特的中国式问候，问候者并非真正想知道对方是否吃了饭，而是一种见面时的客套寒暄。英语国家的人并不会用这种方式打招呼或寒暄，因为在他们看来，这种打招呼方式像是在窥探个人隐私活动。故上述译文没有直译，而是用 pass the time of the day 解释原文的意思。pass the time of the day 在英语中是"寒暄或问好"的意思，语义和原文相符。这里的"吃了吗？"也可以译为：greet each other with a "Hi"，意义、功能同样对等。

译例 4　十字常常写成千字，千字常常写成十字。（胡适《差不多先生传》）

译文　He would mistake the Chinese character 十 (meaning 10) for 千 (meaning 1,000), and vice versa. （张培基 译）

分析 "十"和"千"两个汉字的书写，中国人都非常熟悉，但英语国家读者可能不知道，直译很可能使其无法理解，但"十"和"千"又是极具中国特色的词汇，必须呈现给读者，读者才能明白，这两个字经常互相写错的原因是因为其外形相似。上述译文直接借用了汉字"十"和"千"，再通过括号加注的方式进行解释，从而帮助读者更好地理解原文。

汉英翻译时，有些次要的文化背景可以淡化处理，有时甚至可以省译。本书第 3 讲【真题译·注·评】中的知识点评部分，有相关例子，这里不再重复分析。

真题译·注·评

◆◆◆ 译文对比 ◆◆◆

¹ 家有良田，可能要被水淹掉；家有宫殿，可能要被火烧掉；肚子里有文化，水淹不掉，火烧不掉，谁都拿不走。（合肥工业大学·真题）

² 这句话是我父亲说的。父亲是个农民，只读过一年私塾，是个没文化的人。

译文　① Farmland, however fertile, may be overwhelmed by water; palace, however grand, may be destroyed by fire; knowledge, however, will never be taken away. My father told me that. He is an illiterate farmer with only one-year schooling.

② My father, a farmer, once told me, "fertile land can be flooded and palaces be burned, ³while knowledge is always in your mind and can't be taken away in any case." He only studied in a private school for one year so could hardly read and write.

从小我就生长在农村，很少人会去重视知识的重要性，加上我们乡就只有唯一一所高中，⁴升学率很低。所以，我上完小学就没有好好读书，心想反正上不了高中，⁵破罐子破摔，初中的成绩很差。从来不怎么关心我学习的父亲开始注意到我的状态，对我的学习关心起来。

译文　① I grew up in the countryside where few were aware of the importance of knowledge. And then there was only one high school in my hometown, so most students would hardly have the chance to study further there. I didn't take my study seriously after primary school, thinking it's next to impossible to study at the high school. No hope at all, so it wasn't worth efforts. My score was really poor in the junior middle school. It was at the time that my father began to care about my study. This had never happened before.

1　家有良田，可能要被水淹掉；家有宫殿，可能要被火烧掉。原文结构对称，译文也尽量做到结构对称，译为：Farmland, however fertile, may be overwhelmed by water; palace, however grand, may be destroyed by fire。其中，however grand 是为了结构对称增译的，但也没有画蛇添足，因为宫殿本身就具有"宏伟"的特征。译文实现了"信"的标准。

2　第二段只有一句话，且和前文语义联系紧密、衔接顺畅，故可以与第一段合译。

3　while 强调两者之间的对比关系，而 but 主要表示转折关系。故此处应用 but。

4　"升学率很低"的表述撇开语境，客观来讲偏说明文体，为使译文再现原文文学色彩，可以用带有感情的解释进行翻译，译为：most students would hardly have the chance to study further there。

5　破罐子破摔。英语没有这样的比喻形象，为"信"于原文，故选择意译"No hope at all, so it wasn't worth efforts"。

② I grew up in the countryside. People there seldom realized the importance of knowledge. And it [6]is pretty hard to enter the only high school in my village. With the thought that I was not able to pass the entrance examination anyway, I didn't work hard after graduation from primary school. As a result, my performance at middle school [7]is terrible. My dad, never interested in my study before, began to realize my negative attitude and worry about me.

在乡下，大人和孩子间平时交流很少。在我的印象中，这是父亲第一次找我聊天，时间是我上初三春节的最后一天。第二天就开学了，我要去读初中的最后一学期——可能也是我一生的最后一学期。这次谈话父亲显然有所准备，专门把我叫去几公里外的一所高中，也就是我后来读高中的地方。我们围着学校围墙走，一边走，父亲一边开导我，虚虚实实，深深浅浅，说了很多，其中就有这句话。

译文 ① Children would seldom communicate with their parents in the countryside. As I remember, my father offered to talk with me for the first time on the last day of the third-year winter vacation. The next day, I would go to school for my last semester, or maybe, the last one in my life. He seemed to have prepared for this conversation. He asked me to go to the high school several miles away, the one where I would study later. We talked, walking along the school wall. He said a lot, both simple and profound truth, and tried to persuade me, in a direct or indirect manner, into realizing the importance of study. The initial words were also said then.

② In rural areas, adults seldom [8]communicated with children in daily life. So it's the first time that my dad talked to me so seriously in my memory. It was the last day of Spring Festival holiday during my third year in the middle school. Next day I would go to school for the last semester [9]of learning—probably the last in my whole life. Then I was brought by father to the high school several miles away, the one that I attended later. He had, [10]obviously, well prepared for this conversation. He [11]led us around the school wall and tried to persuade me during our walk. [12]He talked a lot both in a direct and indirect manner. And among those he told me was the above saying.

我后来想，为了这句话，父亲也许想了一夜，也许讨教了某位老师，也许是灵感突发，灵机一动。总之，这句话永远烙在了我心里。改变一个人有时候就是一句话，一夜之间，一念之间。[13]带着这句话上学后，我像换了个人。那年，我顺利地考上了高中。

---

6 讲过去的事情，应用过去式，此处属于时态错误。此外，中学是在乡（hometown），而非村（village），属于误译。

7 讲过去的事情，应用过去式，此处属于时态错误。

8 过去经常做某事或过去经常是某种情况，用 would do 来表示，不用一般过去时。

9 对于学生而言的"学期（semester）"，必定跟学习（learning）相关，故 of learning 多余。

10 obviously 修饰整个句子，要放在句首。

11 led sb. around some place 意为"带领某人参观某地"，与原文意义不符；而且当时只带着我一个人（me），不是 us。

12 这里漏译"深深浅浅"。

13 这一句和文章最后一句衔接更通顺，放在尾段。

译文　① How did my father come up with them? He, I thought, may have racked his brains for a whole night, or got hint from a certain teacher, or it was just out of inspiration. I will remember these words forever. Changes of a person sometimes are made by a single word or a changed mind and this may take place all of a sudden.

② I tried to guess how [14]can my dad speak those words at that time. Maybe he had deliberated for a whole night, maybe he borrowed them from some teachers or maybe all came from a flash of inspiration. [15]No matter how the saying is imprinted in my mind. Sometimes people can [16]change with one sentence, one night or one thought. With the words deeply rooted in my mind, I became totally different and succeeded in the entrance examination the same year.

这是我人生的第一个转折。我现在所有的一切，都是从这里起步的。

译文　① With these words in my mind, I began to immerse myself in study and entered the high school that year. It was my first turning point and everything I have now started from it.

② [17]Attending high school marked the first turning point in my life. All I own now is based on that period of learning.

◆◆◆ 知识点评 ◆◆◆

（1）口语风格的语言特征

原文是一个文学作品的片段，回忆自己的父亲以及自己小时候的学习经历，语言简单朴实，偏口语化。译文也应该做到风格对应，用词简单、句式简单，用简单易懂的语言传达原文的意思。不宜用一些大词、正式词或复杂的句子结构，否则不符合原文的语体特征。译文①通篇都是简单的表达、简单的句式，力求和原文风格一致。

译例 1　从小我就生长在农村，很少人会去重视知识的重要性，加上我们乡就只有唯一一所高中，升学率很低。所以，我上完小学就没有好好读书，心想反正上不了高中，**破罐子破摔**，初中的成绩很差。从来不怎么关心我学习的父亲开始注意到我的状态，对我的学习关心起来。

译文　I grew up in the countryside where few were aware of the importance of knowledge. And then there was only one high school in my hometown, so most students would hardly have the chance to study further there. I didn't take my study seriously after primary school, thinking

---

14　这里应用过去时，can 改为 could。

15　No matter how 的语法功能是引导让步状语从句，无法单独成句。该句不是一个完整句子，属语法错误。

16　change 是及物动词，后面要加宾语，或者也可以改为被动 be changed。而且，"change with one sentence, one night or one thought" 没有可读性，读者可能没法理解。

17　Attending high school marked the first turning point in my life 可以改为 Attending the high school was the first turning point in my life。was 相比 marked 更显静态。

it's next to impossible to study at the high school. <u>No hope at all, so it wasn't worth efforts.</u> My score was really poor in the junior middle school. It was at the time that my father began to care about my study. This had never happened before.

分析 整段译文都是一些简单的单词和句子结构，译文尽量贴近原文风格。此外，口语体不要求每个句子都是完整的、符合标准语法结构的句子。译文中"No hope at all, so it wasn't worth efforts."不是语法错误，反而在忠实原文意义的基础上，再现了原文"破罐子破摔"的口语体风格。

（2）避开非英语表达

使用非英语表达是学生译文常见问题。英语造句要符合单词的用法、搭配以及表达习惯，不能随意编造、随意搭配，这样只会导致译文生硬，甚至出现误译而被扣分。

译例 2 所以，我上完小学就没有好好读书，<u>心想</u>反正上不了高中，破罐子破摔，初中的成绩很差。

译文 ① I didn't take my study seriously after primary school, <u>thinking</u> it's next to impossible to study at the high school. No hope at all, so it wasn't worth efforts.

② <u>With the thought that</u> I was not able to pass the entrance examination anyway, I didn't work hard after graduation from primary school. As a result, my performance at middle school is terrible.

译例 3 拓**在我看来**，文化交流过程中不同文化元素的结合可以使我们的文化更加发达。

译文 ① <u>In my opinion</u>, the combination of different elements in the process of cultural exchange can make our culture more thriving.

② <u>To my mind's eye</u>, the combination of different cultural elements in the process of cultural exchange can make our culture more developed.

分析 译例 2 中，译文②中的 With the thought that... 表面上没有语法错误，但不符合英语的表达习惯，英语用 thinking 一词表达"心想"即可。译例 3 中，To my mind's eye 这种说法在英语中根本不存在，用 In my opinion 即可。

第10讲 文言文的翻译

文言文是中国古代的一种书面语言，长期占有主导地位，五四运动后，其地位逐渐被白话文所取代。文言文注重典故、骈俪对仗、音律工整，包含策、诗、词、曲、八股、骈文等多种文体。

文言文的一个重要特点是行文简练，这和我国古代的记载方式有关。早期人们将文字写在龟壳、木简、竹简之上，由于这些书写载体位置有限，为了尽可能地记录更多的信息，各种成分经常被省略。古文中，省去主语、宾语、谓语、介词的情况很常见。此外，文言文中单音词占优势，双音词和多音词比较少。单音词的使用也是古文表达简洁的一个重要原因。

第 1 节 文言文与现代汉语对比

1.1 词

1.1.1 古今异义

文言文中有的词语古今同义，例如：国号、年号、帝号、官名、地名、人名、器物名、书名、度量衡单位等专有名词。但也有部分文言词语的意义发生了不同程度的变化，古今异义。

有的词语词义扩大，今义的范围大于古义，古义被包括在今义之中。例如，古文中的"皮"指兽皮，现在不仅可以指动植物的皮，也可以指包在外面的一层东西，比如"封皮"。古文中的"江"专指长江，"河"专指黄河，现在"江河"则泛指一切江河。

有的词语词义缩小，今义的范围小于古义。例如，古汉语中的"官"原指官员或官府，后来词义逐渐缩小至官员。在古汉语中，"行李"既可以指出门所带的包裹、箱子等，又可指出使的人。例如，"行李之往来，共其乏困"（《烛之武退秦师》）中的"行李"就指出使的人，而现代汉语中"行李"仅指出门所带的东西。

有些词语的意义加深了，即词义强化。"恨"在古代多表遗憾、不满意。例如，"先帝在时，每与臣论此事，未尝不叹息痛恨于桓灵也"（《出师表》），而在现代汉语中，"恨"则表仇恨、怀恨。

和词义强化相反，有些词语的意义减弱了，即词义弱化。例如，"饥饿"中的"饿"字，古义是指严重的饥饿，已达到死亡威胁的程度。"饿其体肤，空乏其身"（《孟子》）中的"饿"就是古义，而现代汉语中"饿"指一般的肚子饿。"怨恨"的"怨"字，古义即"恨"，而今天的"怨"由古义"恨"减弱为"不满意、责备"的意思，如"任劳任怨"。

有些词语意义完全发生了变化，即词义转移。例如，"弃甲曳兵而走"（《寡人之于国也》）中的"走"，古义是"跑，逃跑"，今天是"一步步地走"的意思。"以暴露百姓之骨于中原"（《勾践灭吴》）中的"中原"，古义指原野，而现在则指中原地区。

还有些文言词语的感情色彩发生了变化。如："先帝不以臣卑鄙"（《出师表》）中的"卑"指地位低下，"鄙"指知识浅陋，是用于自谦的褒义词语，而当今的"卑鄙"则指品质恶劣，其意义已完全转变为贬义。

1.1.2 一词多义

古文以单音词为主，而现代汉语则以双音词为主。例如，"齐师伐我，公将战"（《左传·曹刿论战》），七个字就是七个词。而现代汉语里，这些单音词都变成了相应的双音词：齐——齐国，师——军队，伐——攻打，我——我国，公——庄公，将——就要，战——迎战。

对单音词来说，由于缺少搭配限制，往往具有多个义项，其意义在不同的句子中有不同的理解。以"故"为例：

温故而知新，可以为师矣。（旧的知识）《论语》

广故数言欲亡。（故意）《陈涉世家》

公问其故。（原因）《曹刿论战》

而两狼之并驱如故。（原样）《狼》

桓侯故使人问之。（特意）《扁鹊见蔡桓公》

由此可见，词语的理解一定要结合语境，词不离句，甚至词不离段、词不离篇。

随着汉语的发展，单音词逐渐双音化，使词语同音的现象大大减少了。例如，"蚤"和"早"同音，但"跳蚤"和"早晨"并不同音；"伐、乏、罚"同音，但"征伐、缺乏、处罚"却不同音。单音词的双音化有效地节制了一词多义的滋生和发展。例如，"文"在古文中，有"花纹、文采、文章、文学、文字、文献、文饰"等不同意义，属于一词多义，但双音化后的"花纹""文饰"则是特定意义，不属于一词多义。

古文一词多义不仅和语境有关，还和词的本义、引申义、比喻义和假借义有关。

词的本义，就是词的本来意义，即词产生时最初的意义。如"本"的本义是"草木的根"，"道"的本义是"路途、道路"。

词的引申义，就是词由本义派生出的与本义相关的其他意义。如"道"的本义为"路途、道路"，其引申义为"方向、方法、道理"；"本"的本义为"草木的根"，其引申义为"根本、本来、原本、基本"。"孟尝君至关，关法鸡鸣而出客"中的"关"本指"门闩"，由于作用相似，引申为"关卡"。

词的比喻义，就是在比喻基础上所产生的意义。如"爪牙"的本义是"鸟兽的爪子和牙齿"，比喻义是"得力的帮手或武士"，属褒义词，而现多比喻"为坏人效力的人或党羽"，属贬义词；"草菅人命"中的"草菅"，本义是"野草"，比喻义是"不值得珍惜的事物"。

词的假借义，就是因假借而产生的含义。古文中常常出现通假现象。"通假"就是"通用、借代"的意思，即用读音或字形相同或者相近的字代替本字。（此处简要提及，后面【1.1.4 善用通假】中会对此详细讲解）

总的来说，一词多义是古今汉语所共有的现象，但古汉语更加普遍，义项也往往更多。

1.1.3 文言虚词

人们常说"之、乎、也、者、矣、焉、哉，用得妙了是秀才"。文言虚词指没有实际意义的词，在文言文中一般不作句子成分。例如，"陈胜者，阳城人也"。"者……也"表判断，无义，理解时可删去。这个句子可以理解为：陈胜是阳城人。

虚词主要分为介词、连词、助词以及语气词四大类。相比现代汉语，少数虚词用法延续了下来，如"学不可以已"（《劝学》）中的"可以"古今意义相同。也有一些虚词在现代汉语中完全消失，如发语词"夫""盖"，语气词"矣""哉"等。也有一些虚词古今意义不同，例如，"此先汉所以兴隆也"（《出师表》）中的"所以"意为"……的原因"，而在现代汉语中表示"结果"的意思。

相比现代汉语，古文虚词用法往往更为灵活，意义更广，而且横跨多个词类。以"而"为例，其主要用法如下：

（1）用作连词。可连接词、短语和分句，表示多种关系。

①表示并列关系。如：**蟹六跪而二螯**。《劝学》

②表示递进关系。如：**君子博学而日参省乎己**。《劝学》

③表示承接关系，意为"就"或"接着"。如：**余方心动欲还，而大声发于水上**。《石钟山记》

④表示转折关系。如：**青，取之于蓝，而青于蓝**。《劝学》

⑤表示假设关系。如：**诸君而有意，瞻予马首可也**。《冯婉贞》

（2）用作代词。只用作第二人称，一般作定语，意为"你的"。

例如：**而翁长铨，迁我京职，则汝朝夕侍母**。《记王忠肃公翱事》

（3）复音虚词"而已"，置于句末，相当于"罢了"。

例如：**一人、一桌、一椅、一扇、一抚尺而已**。《口技》

要想读懂古文，理解文言虚词是非常重要的。理解文言虚词一定要结合语境，根据逻辑推断虚词的语法意义和词汇意义，一旦脱离句子或上下文就无从理解。

1.1.4　善用通假

【1.1.2　一词多义】中曾提到：古文以单音词为主。单音词占优势，同音词自然就多。众多的同音词为"同音代替"提供了便利，古文里那么多通假字，是和单音词占优势这种状况分不开的。

现代汉语的正式文体中已较少使用通假字，而在古代的文言文中通假字是常见现象。"通假"就是"通用、借代"的意思，即用读音或字形相同或者相近的字代替本字。如，《论语六则》中"学而时习之，不亦说乎？"的"说"通"悦"，表示"愉快"的意思；《木兰诗》中"著我旧时裳"的"著"通"着"，表示"穿"的意思。古人造出一个字，表达一个意思，可是该用哪个字表示哪个意思，最初用法没有一定规范，既可以使用这个字表示某个意思，又可以使用另外一个读音相同或者相近的字表示同一个意思。所以，时代越早的文章，通假字越多。

另外，由于古代印刷相对落后，加之战火焚毁，相当一部分书籍在原版遗失后，是凭一些读书人的背诵、记忆重新写出来的。由于一时记不清、查不到本字，这些人可能会临时借用音同或音近的字来代替，或只图省事而有意写了笔画较少的音同、音近或形似的别字。后来这些"代替字"、"别字"得以沿用，成了通假字。

怎样辨析古文中的通假字？一个字如果本义和引申义都解释不通，便可从字音相同或相近方面寻求本字。例如：《陈涉世家》中"为天下唱，宜多应者"，"唱"通"倡"。也可以凭借字形，辨析通假。例如：《国殇》中"操吴戈兮被犀甲"，"被"通"披"；《赤壁之战》中"五万兵难卒合"，"卒"通"猝"，意为：五万兵难在仓猝之间集合起来。

1.2　句

文言句式与现代汉语句式基本相同。它们都分单句和复句，都有"主谓宾"和"定状补"六大成分，句子的语序也基本相同。但是，由于文言文有些实词和现代汉语用法不同，因此就出现了一些特殊句式——判断句、被动句、省略句、倒装句。想学好文言文的翻译，掌握文言特殊句式，正确理解句子含义非常必要。

1.2.1 判断句

判断句是对人物或事物的性质、情况做出判断的句子，常用表达如下：

（1）用"者……也"表判断

例如：

①廉颇者，赵之良将也。（司马迁《廉颇蔺相如列传》）

②陈胜者，阳城人也。（司马迁《陈涉世家》）

③师者，所以传道受业解惑也。（韩愈《师说》）

（2）句末用"者也"表判断

①城北徐公，齐国之美丽者也。（《战国策·邹忌讽齐王纳谏》）

②予谓菊，花之隐逸者也；牡丹，花之富贵者也；莲，花之君子者也。（周敦颐《爱莲说》）

（3）用"者"表判断

四人者，庐陵萧君圭君玉，长乐王回深父，余弟安国平父，安上纯父。（王安石《游褒禅山记》）

（4）用动词"为"或判断词"是"表判断

①马超、韩遂尚在关西，为操后患。（司马光《赤壁之战》）

②同行十二年，不知木兰是女郎。（北朝民歌《木兰诗》）

③同是天涯沦落人，相逢何必曾相识。（白居易《琵琶行》）

（5）用"即、乃、则、皆、本、诚、亦、素、必"等副词表示肯定判断

①此诚危急存亡之秋也。（诸葛亮《出师表》）

②此则岳阳楼之大观也。（范仲淹《岳阳楼记》）

③且相如素贱人。（司马迁《廉颇蔺相如列传》）

④鱼，我所欲也；熊掌，亦我所欲也。（孟子《鱼我所欲也》）

（6）用"非"表示否定判断

①子非我，安知我不知鱼之乐？（庄子《秋水》）

②六国破灭，非兵不利，战不善，弊在赂秦。（苏洵《六国论》）

③城非不高也，池非不深也，兵革非不坚利也……（孟子《孟子·公孙丑下》）

（7）无标志判断句

文言文中的判断句有时没有任何标志，直接由"名词对名词"做出判断。例如：

刘备天下枭雄。（司马光《赤壁之战》）

1.2.2 被动句

被动句有两大类型：有标志被动句和无标志被动句。

古代汉语中，有标志被动句式主要有四种：

（1）用"于"表示被动关系

用介词"于"引出行为的主动者，"于"置于动词后，形式是："动词＋于＋主动者"。例如："王建禽于秦"中的"于"用在动词"禽"（通"擒"）的后边，引出动作行为的主动者"秦"，表示被动，意为：（齐王）建被秦国擒住。

（2）用"见"表示被动关系

在动词前用"见"或又在动词后加"于"引进主动者。形式是："见＋动词"或者"见＋动词＋于＋主动者"。例如：

①秦城恐不可得，徒<u>见欺</u>。（司马迁《廉颇蔺相如列传》）

②臣恐<u>见欺于王</u>而负赵。（司马迁《廉颇蔺相如列传》）

（3）用"为"表示被动关系

"为"置于动词前表示被动。形式是："为＋动词"、"为＋主动者＋动词"或者"为＋主动者＋所＋动词"。例如：

①若背其言，臣死，妻子<u>为戮</u>，无益于君。《左传》

②茅屋<u>为秋风所破</u>（杜甫《茅屋为秋风所破歌》）

③吴广素爱人，士卒多<u>为用</u>者。（司马迁《陈涉世家》）

④今不速往，恐<u>为操所先</u>。（司马光《赤壁之战》）

⑤有如此之势，而<u>为秦人积威之所劫</u>。（苏洵《六国论》）

⑥不者，若属皆且<u>为所虏</u>。（司马迁《鸿门宴》）

（4）用"被"、"受……于"表示被动关系

形式是："被＋动词"或者"受＋动词＋于＋主动者"。例如：

①信而见疑，忠而<u>被谤</u>，能无怨乎？（司马迁《屈原列传》）

②予犹记周公之<u>被逮</u>，在丁卯三月之望。（张溥《五人墓碑记》）

③吾不能举全吴之地，十万之众，<u>受制于人</u>。（司马光《赤壁之战》）

除了以上有标志被动句，古汉语中也有无标志被动句，即不含被动词的被动句，也叫作意念被动句。例如：

①荆州之民附操者，<u>逼兵势耳</u>（是被兵势所逼的）。《资治通鉴》

②<u>蔓草犹不可除</u>（蔓延的野草尚且不易被铲除），况君之宠弟乎？《左传·郑伯克段于鄢》

1.2.3　省略句

古今汉语都有成分省略，但在古汉语中，省略现象更为普遍。以下例句中，括号内均为省略的成分。

（1）主语的省略

例如：

永州之野产异蛇，（蛇）黑质而白章；（蛇）触草木，（草木）尽死；（蛇）以啮人，（人）无御之者。（柳宗元《捕蛇者说》）

（2）谓语的省略

例如：

①夫战，勇气也。一鼓作气，再（鼓）而衰，三（鼓）而竭……《曹刿论战》

②择其善者而从之，（择）其不善者而改之。《论语》

（3）修饰语和中心词（被修饰对象）的省略

例如：

①吾妻之美我者，私我也；（吾）妾之美我者，畏我也；（吾）客之美我者，欲有求于我也。

《邹忌讽齐王纳谏》

②行一不义（事），杀一无罪（人），而得天下，不为也。《荀子》

（4）介词和介词宾语的省略

例如：

①死马且买之（以）五百金，况生马乎？《千金市马》

②臣与将军戮力而攻秦，将军战（于）河南，臣战（于）河北。（司马迁《鸿门宴》）

③试与他虫斗，虫尽靡。又试之（以）鸡，果如臣言。（蒲松龄《促织》）

④且日，客从外来，与（其）坐谈。《邹忌讽齐王纳谏》

1.2.4　倒装句

（1）主谓倒装

有些感叹句或疑问句，为了表达一种强烈的情感，通常会把谓语置于主语之前，以示强调。

例如：

快哉此风！《黄州快哉亭记》

分析　此句正常语序为：此风快哉！意为：这风真畅快啊。此处谓语提前不仅凸显了"风之快"，还突出了言语者轻快、畅意的心境。

（2）宾语前置

例如：

①**沛公安在**？（司马迁《鸿门宴》）

分析　正常语序应为"沛公在安？"，表示"沛公在哪里？"。"安"意为"哪里"，作介词"在"的宾语。根据古文语法，文言文中用疑问代词"谁""何""奚""安"等作宾语时，往往把宾语放在动词或介词的前面。

②**时人莫之许也**。（陈寿《三国志·诸葛亮传》）

分析　否定句中，代词作宾语，宾语一般前置处理。该例中，此句为否定句，句中代词"之"作动词"许"的宾语，故属于宾语前置类型，其意为：当时人们都不承认这件事。

（3）状语后置

文言文中，介词短语作状语往往后置。例如：

①**申之以孝悌之义**。《寡人之于国也》

②**何不试之以足**？《郑人买履》

分析　例①中，"以孝悌之义"为介词短语后置，正常语序应为：以孝悌之义申之，意为：反复对百姓进行孝敬父母和敬爱兄长的教育。例②同理，"以足"后置，正常语序应为"何不以足试之？"，意为：为什么不用脚去试一试呢？

以上四种文言特殊句式在文言文中很是常见，它们的使用丰富了文言文的表达方式，但同时也增加了阅读难度。了解这些特殊句式的结构和用法，对于理解、翻译文言文具有重要意义。

第 2 节 文言文翻译步骤

2.1 原文灵活分段

在古代中国，文言文大多是不分段的。但在英译古文时，对原文分段翻译是必要之举。如果不分段，段落会显得冗长，读者不易抓住重点，阅读体验不好。翻译文言文时，可以灵活使用三种方法进行分段：对话分段、主题分段和时间分段。

2.1.1 对话分段

文言文中出现对话时，讲话主语会发生变化。当主语发生变化时，可以另起一段。

例 1 孔子适齐，中路闻哭者之声，其音甚哀，孔子下车，追而问曰："子何人也？" // 对曰："吾、丘吾子也"。// 曰："子今非丧之所，奚哭之悲也？" // 丘吾子曰："吾有三失，晚而自觉，悔之何及！" // 曰："三失可得闻乎？愿子告吾，无隐也。" // 丘吾子曰："吾少时好学，周遍天下，后还丧吾亲，是一失也；长事齐君，君骄奢失士，臣节不遂，是二失也；吾平生厚交，而今皆离绝，是三失也。夫树欲静而风不停，子欲养而亲不待。往而不来者、年也；不可再见者、亲也。请从此辞。"遂投水而死。// 孔子曰："小子识之！斯足为戒矣"。自是弟子辞归养亲者十有三。（南京大学·真题）

分析 原文只有一段，但在汉英翻译时可以把原文分为若干段（// 为分段标记）。原文故事主要围绕孔子和丘吾子的对话展开。每逢讲话主语发生变化，均可以分段。对话分段使故事情节更有层次，内容更加清晰，便于读者阅读。如果不分段，段落会显得臃肿，内容揉成一团，增加读者理解的难度。

2.1.2 主题分段和时间分段

英译文言文时，当叙述视角或主题发生变化，可以开始一个新的段落。另外，描述故事时，可以按时间先后分段。

例 2 唐贞元中，扬州坊市间，忽有一妓（明抄本妓作技）术丐乞者，不知所从来。自称姓胡，名媚儿，所为颇甚怪异。旬日之后，观者稍稍云集。其所丐求，日获千万。// 一旦，怀中出一琉璃瓶子，可受半升。表里烘明，如不隔物，遂置于席上。初谓观者曰：有人施与满此瓶子，则足矣。瓶口刚如苇管大。有人与之百钱，投之，琤然有声，则见瓶间大如粟粒，众皆异之。复有人与之千钱，投之如前。又有与万钱者，亦如之。俄有好事人，与之十万二十万，皆如之。或有以马驴入之瓶中，见人马皆如蝇大，动行如故。// 须臾，有度支两税纲，自扬子院，部轻货数十车至。驻观之，以其一时入，或终不能致将他物往，且谓官物不足疑者。乃谓媚儿曰：尔能令诸车皆入此中乎？// 媚儿曰：许之则可。纲曰：且试之。// 媚儿乃微侧瓶口，大喝，诸车辘辘相继，悉入瓶，瓶中历历如行蚁然。有顷，渐不见，媚儿即跳身入瓶中。纲乃大惊，遽取扑破，求之一无所有。从此失媚儿所在。// 后月余日，有人于清河北，逢媚儿，部领车乘，趋东平而去。是时，李师道为东平帅也。《太平广记·胡媚儿》

分析 原文讲的是胡媚儿以怪异的法术为割据东平的藩镇骗取朝廷货物的故事（本故事白话文译文在下面【2.2　语内翻译和语际翻译】部分提供）。原文不分段，理解起来较为困难，英译时则可以根据主题变化、时间先后和对话分成六段。第①段对胡媚儿进行介绍；第②段以"一旦"（一天早上）开头，具体描述当天发生的事情，叙述对象发生了变化，所以另起一段；第③段有明显的时间分段标记"须臾"（不久），讲述了不久后发生在押运货物的官员和胡媚儿之间的事情；第④段属于对话分段；第⑤段讲述了官员同意对方要求后，朝廷货物被骗走的经过；第⑥段也有明显的时间分段标记"后月余日"（一个月之后），讲述了一个月后发生的事情。译文分段描述使段落主题和故事脉络更加清晰，给读者带来更好的阅读体验。

2.2　语内翻译和语际翻译

　　语内翻译指某一种语言内部的转换。方言与民族共同语，方言与方言，古代语与现代语之间的语言转换，都属于语内翻译。而语际翻译指不同语言之间的转换，也就是用一种语言文字表达另外一种语言文字表达的意思。语际翻译就是我们平时所说狭义上的翻译。

　　由于文言文为古汉语，距离现在年代较为久远，对汉语母语者来说理解起来都有一定难度，更不用说英美国家读者。故英译文言文通常涉及语内翻译和语际翻译两个步骤。英译文言文时，一般要先把古汉语转换成现代汉语，再把现代汉语译成英语。当然，并不是说参加翻译硕士考试时，要把文言文对应的现代汉语先写下来。但是，在考生脑海中的确存在语内翻译这个过程，即用现代汉语解读原文的意思。要做好文言文的翻译，首先语内翻译工作要做好，即准确理解原文的意思，其次需要好的语际翻译，即用符合目的语表达习惯的语言把原文意思传达出来。

译例（注：以下例子，原文已根据上述分段方法，分段展示）

　　①唐贞元中，扬州坊市间，忽有一妓（明抄本妓作技）术丐乞者，不知所从来。自称姓胡，名媚儿，所为颇甚怪异。旬日之后，观者稍稍云集。其所丐求，日获千万。

汉译 唐代贞元年间，扬州的街道上，忽然出现一个靠幻术行乞的女艺人，无人知道她来自哪里。她自称姓胡，叫媚儿，表演的幻术十分怪异。十多天后，观众越来越多，每天获利以万计。

英译 Sometime during the reign of Emperor Dezong of Tang, a woman vagrant became a phenomenon in the streets of Yangzhou City. Nobody knew where she came from or who she was, except that her name was Hu Meir. Anyway, that was how she introduced herself. She made a living by performing magic arts, and her arts were rather outlandish. In a fortnight, as her name spread, a permanent crowd gathered around her. In that way she earned tens of thousands a day.

　　②一旦，怀中出一琉璃瓶子，可受半升。表里烘明，如不隔物，遂置于席上。初谓观者曰：有人施与满此瓶子，则足矣。瓶口刚如苇管大。有人与之百钱，投之，然有声，则见瓶间大如粟粒，众皆异之。复有人与之千钱，投之如前。又有与万钱者琤亦如之。俄有好事人，与之十万二十万，皆如之。或有以马驴入之瓶中，见人马皆如蝇大，动行如故。

汉译　一天早晨，她从怀中掏出一个玻璃瓶子，可容半升，表里通明，仿佛中间什么也没有。她把瓶子放在席子上，对观众说："如果有人施舍的钱能够填满这个瓶子，我今后就不再乞讨了。"这个瓶子的口有芦苇杆那么大。有人拿出一百钱，向瓶子里投去，当当作响，钱进入瓶中，只有米粒大小。大家都很吃惊。又有人给媚儿一千钱，跟刚才一样投进瓶中，结果同前面一样。又有给一万钱的，结果也是一样。一会儿有个好事者，投入十几、二十万钱，结果还是一样。还有将驴马赶入瓶子里的，驴马全都变得苍蝇大小，动作还是原来的样子。

英译　One morning, she retrieved from the folds of her garment a glass bottle. It was transparent and one could see through it. She placed it on the straw mat and announced that if someone could fill it she would not need to beg any more. It was not a big bottle, about the size of a half-liter jar with a neck no thicker than a reed stem. Someone offered a hundred coins. One could hear the coins clinking to the bottom, but once inside the bottle they looked as small as grains of rice. The audience was fascinated. Another came up with a thousand coins, and still another dropped in ten thousand. Then a dude jingled in a hundred thousand and the bottle was no fuller than it had been. Horses and donkeys were driven in, and they shrank to the size of bugs, but still plodding along as if nothing had happened.

③须臾，有度支两税纲，自扬子院，部轻货数十车至。驻观之，以其一时入，或终不能致将他物往，且谓官物不足疑者。乃谓媚儿曰：尔能令诸车皆入此中乎？

汉译　不久，有个掌财政的税官，从扬子院押运几十车货物路过这里，停下来观看，心想就算货物一时进入瓶中，她也不可能把货物运往别的地方，况且这是皇家的财物，不用担心。他对胡媚儿说："你能让这些车辆都进瓶子里吗？"

英译　Before long, a high official from the Revenue Department came along with a caravan of several dozen wagons loaded with local produce on their way to the capital. The official stopped to watch. She could by no means carry off the heavily guarded caravan under his nose, he thought, not to say that this was royal property. "Can you transport my whole caravan into your bottle?" he challenged.

④媚儿曰：许之则可。纲曰：且试之。

汉译　胡媚儿说："只要允许就可以。"税官说："你可以试一下。"

英译　"With your permission," she replied succinctly, and he gave his consent.

⑤媚儿乃微侧瓶口，大喝，诸车辘辘相继，悉入瓶，瓶中历历如行蚁然。有顷，渐不见，媚儿即跳身入瓶中。纲乃大惊，遽取扑破，求之一无所有。从此失媚儿所在。

汉译　胡媚儿就微侧瓶口，大吼一声，那些车辆便滚滚向前，相继进入瓶中。车辆在瓶子里就像爬行的蚂蚁一样。一会儿，便看不见了。这时，只见胡媚儿纵身一跃，跳入瓶中。税官大惊，当即抓起瓶子摔碎，结果什么也没有。从此，大家都不知道胡媚儿的下落。

英译　Tilting the bottle slightly, she let out a loud hoot. The whole caravan rumbled ahead into the bottle like a line of crawling ants. Slowly, the wagons faded from sight. Before the astonished official realized what was happening, she herself jumped into the bottle. He grabbed the bottle and smashed it on the ground. There was nothing in it.

⑥后月余日，有人于清河北，逢媚儿，部领车乘，趋东平而去。是时，李师道为东平帅也。《太平广记·胡媚儿》

汉译　一个多月后，在清河北面，有人看见胡媚儿领着那些车辆，朝东平而去。当时，李师道正在东平的军队担任主将。

英译　A month later, someone saw Meir in Qinghe county, hundreds of miles to the north of Yangzhou, leading a wagon-train in the direction of Dongping, the capital of warlord Li Shidao.

（张光前 译）

分析　上例，在理解原文基础上，先语内翻译后语际翻译。其中，语内翻译是语际翻译的基础，前者的准确与否直接决定了语际翻译在内容上是否忠实原文。

　　要做好语内翻译，不仅要了解古文的词法和句法，还要了解其写作背景、写作目的、主题以及句间逻辑，从而准确地抓住原文信息。要做好语际翻译，在掌握英语单词用法、语法的基础上，还要了解英语的表达习惯以及中英文的区别，从而产出一个准确、地道的译文。

第 3 节　文言文翻译技巧

文言文英译和现代汉语英译有很多相似之处，比如增加连接词以体现句间逻辑关系。但由于文言文有些句法结构与现代汉语不同，比如多用倒装、省略以及文言虚词，文言文翻译也有不同之处。文言文翻译需灵活使用三种技巧：增译、省译和合译。

3.1　增译

由于文言文多省略和善意合的文体特征，要想向现代读者传达原文的完整意义、传递完整的文言文故事情节，很多时候都需要增译处理。例如，增译省略结构中省略的成分、增译意合文体中缺少的连词以及增译一些起衔接作用的内容。

3.1.1　增译省略成分

古文常省略各种成分，如主语、谓语、宾语等。对于这些省略成分，翻译时，可以根据译文理解需要，予以补上。

译例 1 吾妻之美我者，私我也；（吾）妾之美我者，畏我也；（吾）客之美我者，欲有求于我也。《邹忌讽齐王纳谏》

汉译 我的妻子认为我美，是偏爱我；我的小妾认为我美，是惧怕我；我的客人认为我美，是想要有求于我。

英译 My wife told me that I was handsome, because she was partial to me. My concubine told me the same, because she feared me. My guest echoed the praise, because he wanted to ask me a favour. （谢百魁 译）

分析 原文包含三个分句，有两处省略了修饰词"吾"（原文以括号标示）。英译时，将三个分句译成三个独立的主从复合句。后两个省略修饰词的分句在翻译时，为了补充句子主语的身份信息，均增译 My。如果不增译，直接使用可数名词单数作主语，缺乏限定词，不仅意义不明，而且属于语法错误。

译例 2 生乎吾前（者），其闻道也固先乎吾，吾从而师之；生乎吾后（者），其闻道也亦先乎吾，吾从而师之。《师说》

汉译 生在我前面的人，懂得道理本来就早于我，我应该跟他学习；生在我后面的人，如果懂得道理也早于我，我也应该跟他学习。

英译 Anyone who was born before me and learned the doctrine before me is my teacher. Anyone who was born after me but learned the doctrine before me is also my teacher. （罗经国 译）

分析 原文有两处省略中心词（被修饰的对象）"者"。两处在翻译时均增译 Anyone，以体现句子讨论的对象。若不增译，按照原文结构直译，译文可能会存在语法问题。

译例 3 巫医乐师百工之人，君子不齿，今其智乃反不能及（之），其可怪也欤！《师说》

汉译 巫医、乐师和各种工匠，君子们不屑一顾，现在他们的智慧反而比不上那些人，真是令人奇怪啊！

英译 Medicine men, musicians and handicrafts men are despised by the gentlemen. How strange it is that gentlemen are less wise than these people!（罗经国 译）

分析 原文省略了动词"及"后面的宾语"之"，后者指代前面提到的"巫医、乐师和各种工匠"。英语译文增译了 these people，和 gentlemen 形成对比，再现了原文的比较关系。但是，翻译方法并不是唯一的，原文省略的成分在译文中并不一定需要增译。杨宪益、戴乃迭就将上句译为"Physicians, musicians and artisans are despised by gentlemen, yet they seem to be more intelligent. Is this not strange?"，在不增译的情况下，同样传达了原文的意思。由此可见，对于文言文中的省略结构，增译只是其中一个选择。

3.1.2 增译连词

汉语是意合的语言，句间逻辑往往暗含在字里行间，不需要借用连词来彰显。相比现代汉语，古文意合更加普遍。而英语是形合的语言，句间逻辑往往通过连词来体现。所以，英译文言文时，往往需要将句间隐含的逻辑关系找出，再用恰当的连词表现出来。

译例 4 嗟乎！师道之不传也久矣！欲人之无惑也难矣！《师说》

汉译 唉，古代从师学习的风尚已经很久不流传了，想要人没有疑惑难啊！

英译 Alas, since men have long ceased learning from teachers, it is hard not to be ignorant.

（杨宪益、戴乃迭 译）

分析 从师学习的风尚很久不流传，所以大家普遍都存在困惑，二者之间存在因果关系。译文增译 since，把句间因果关系体现出来。

译例 5 狡兔死，走狗烹；飞鸟尽，良弓藏；敌国破，谋臣亡。《资治通鉴·汉纪三》

汉译 狡猾的兔子被杀死了，驱赶追逐兔子的猎狗也会被拿来烹煮；天上的飞鸟抓完了，好的弓箭也只能收起来；敌国一破，出谋划策的臣子也难免一死。

英译 When the cunning hares are killed, the good hound is thrown into the cauldron; when the soaring birds have been caught, the good bow is put away; when enemy states are overthrown, the wise minister is killed.

分析 当狡兔死，走狗就会被烹；当飞鸟尽，良弓就会被藏起来；当敌国被灭，谋臣就会被杀死。原文不需要用"当"就能传达句间逻辑。但英语是形合的语言，译文增译三个 when，把句间逻辑体现出来，否则英语读者不一定能识别句间的逻辑联系。

译例 6 父母在，不远游，游必有方。《论语·里仁》

汉译 父母在世，不出远门，如果要出远门，必须告知父母自己所去的地方。

英译 While his parents are alive, the son should not travel far away. If he does need to do so, his parents must be informed of the exact place he will go to.

分析 "父母在，不远游"意为"当父母在世的时候，儿子不应该去遥远的地方"，"当"这一连词在原文中没有出现。"游必有方"意为"如果真的要出远门，必须告诉父母去的地方"，"如果"在原文中也没有出现。译文则根据英语表达习惯，分别增译 While 和 If，准确地再现了原文的句间逻辑。

3.1.3　增译其他

当原文讲述一个故事的时候，译者有时可以灵活添加一些信息，从而使语言更加通顺，内容更加生动，译文的可读性更强。

译例 7　丘吾子曰："吾有三失，晚而自觉，悔之何及！"曰："三失可得闻乎？愿子告吾，无隐也。"丘吾子曰："吾少时好学，周遍天下，后还丧吾亲，是一失也；长事齐君，君骄奢失士，臣节不遂，是二失也；吾平生厚交，而今皆离绝，是三失也。夫树欲静而风不停，子欲养而亲不待。往而不来者、年也；不可再见者、亲也。请从此辞。"遂投水而死。// 孔子曰："小子识之！斯足为戒矣"。自是弟子辞归养亲者十有三。

汉译　……话音刚落，这个悲痛的男子便跳水而死。

孔子说："你们要记住他讲的话，以这件事为教训"。之后的几年里，有十三个弟子辞别孔子，回家陪伴父母。

英译　...After saying these words, the grieved man jumped into the water, leaving the world.

Seeing this, Confucius turned around, telling his students, "You should remember his words as a lesson." In the following years, thirteen of his students left him to accompany and support their parents.

分析　丘吾子讲完他的"三失"后，因为过于悲痛，跳河自杀。孔子看到这一幕，告诉他的学生要引以为戒。我们可以想象下当时的情形：孔子和丘吾子对话，当时学生很可能站在他的后面。当丘吾子投河后，孔子很可能是先转过头，再对他的学生讲话的。所以，译文增加了"Confucius turned around"这一动作，这使得故事画面更连贯，叙述更顺畅，在读者脑海中出现的是一个完整的、前后衔接的画面。如果不增译，丘吾子跳水和孔子告诫学生两件事情的衔接不是很顺。

译例 8　兖州徂徕山寺曰光化，客有习儒业者，坚志栖焉。// 夏日凉天，因阅壁画于廊序。忽逢白衣美女，年十五六，姿貌绝异。// 客询其来，笑而应曰："家在山前。"《太平广记·光化寺客》

汉译　兖州徂徕山上有一个叫光化寺的寺庙，有一个儒生住在里面刻苦学习。

夏季，有一天天气非常凉爽，儒生正在欣赏墙上的壁画，突然碰到一个十五六岁的白衣美女。

儒生询问她来自哪里。对方笑着回答"家就在山前"。

英译　Far away from worldly hustle and bustle, up on Culai Mountain was a Buddhist temple named Guanghua. Once, a young man of the Confucian school took up residence there to concentrate on his books, brushing up for the imperial examinations.

One cool summer day while he was perusing the murals on the temple walls, he bumped into a beautiful girl in pure white about sixteen years of age.

"Never seen you around here," he said admiringly. " Are your from afar?"

"No. I live just down the hill," she smiled back.

（张光前 译）

分析　上述译文有三处增译。原文一开始交代故事发生的地点——徂徕山光化寺。译文增译 Far away from worldly hustle and bustle 有助于渲染气氛，凸显故事地点的幽静，而且 hustle and bustle 押尾韵，读起来朗朗上口，具有一种音韵美和节奏美。虽然山上寺庙本就远离喧嚣，但这一增译并没有画蛇添足，因为译文巧妙外显了原文背景暗含的信息，更能凸显故事氛围。

第二处增译是 brushing up for the imperial examinations。古代大多数儒生读书的目的是参加政府举办的科举考试，考取功名，增译这一信息不仅使故事描述更加具体，内容更加丰富，也可以向读者传达相关的文化背景知识。

第三处增译是 admiringly。儒生在寺庙欣赏壁画时，见一美貌女子，顿生心动，增译 admiringly 还原了儒生当时的爱慕之情，也使故事描述更加生动形象，以引起读者阅读兴趣。

译例 9　唐贞元中，扬州坊市间，忽有一妓（明抄本妓作技）术丐乞者，不知所从来。自称姓胡，名媚儿，所为颇甚怪异。旬日之后，观者稍稍云集。其所丐求，日获千万。

《太平广记·胡媚儿》

汉译　唐代贞元年间，扬州的街道上，忽然出现一个靠幻术行乞的女艺人，无人知道她来自哪里。她自称姓胡，叫媚儿，表演的幻术十分怪异。十多天后，观众越来越多，每天获利以万计。

英译　Sometime during the reign of Emperor Dezong of Tang, a woman vagrant became a phenomenon in the streets of Yangzhou City. Nobody knew where she came from or who she was, except that her name was Hu Meir. Anyway, that was how she introduced herself. She made a living by performing magic arts, and her arts were rather outlandish. In a fortnight, as her name spread, a permanent crowd gathered around her. In that way she earned tens of thousands a day.（张光前 译）

分析　此例中，增译 In that way 是为了译文的通顺。"In a fortnight, as her name..." 和 "she earned tens of thousands a day." 语义不够连贯。前一句讲到"随着名声越来越大，在她旁边聚集了越来越多的观众"，后一句提到"每天获利以万计"。"观众多"和"获利"并不存在明显的语义关联。增译 In that way，指代前面的 performing magic arts。观众越来越多→为他们表演魔术→挣上一大笔钱，三件事情具有语义联系。如果不增译 In that way，前后句衔接不够顺畅，影响了语言的流利和故事的可读性。

3.2　省译

古文虚词使用较多，而虚词一般只起"助词"作用，没有实质意义，翻译时一般可以省去不译。此外，故事中有些次要的文化背景不是读者关注的焦点，有时也可以省译。

3.2.1　省译虚词

译例 10　师道之不传也久矣！欲人之无惑也难矣！《师说》

汉译　古代从师学习的风尚已经很久不流传了，想要人没有疑惑难啊！

英译　The tradition of learning from the teacher has long been neglected. Thus it is difficult to find a person without any doubts at all.（罗经国 译）

分析　原文使用了三个虚词"之""也"和"矣"。"之"是结构助词，放在主谓之间，起取消句子独立性的作用（"师道不传"是主谓结构，可以看作一个句子。加"之"则变成一个短语，而非句子），没有实质意义。"也"在这里是语气助词，表示停顿，以舒缓语气，没有实质意义。"矣"用在句末，表示陈述，相当于"了"，也没有实质意义。在原文中没有实质意义的虚词，在翻译时可以省译。

译例11 闻道有先后，术业有专攻，如是而已。《师说》

汉译 懂得道理有先有后，各有各在某行业擅长的技能，就这样罢了。

英译 The fact is that one might have learned the doctrine earlier than the other, or might be a master in his own special field.（罗经国 译）

分析 "而"可以作音节助词，常与其他虚词连用构成复音虚词，比如"而已"。"而已"放在句末相当于"罢了"，没有实质意义。"如是而已"可以理解为"就这样罢了"。译文省译"而已"，将"如是"译为 the fact，后面用同位语从句对其进行解释。

译例12 居庙堂之高则忧其民，处江湖之远则忧其君。《岳阳楼记》

汉译 在朝廷里做高官就担忧他的百姓，身处偏远的地方就担忧他的君王。

英译 When such men are high in the government, their first concern is for the people; when they retire to distant streams and lakes, their first concern is for the sovereign.（杨宪益、戴乃迭 译）

分析 原文"之"是结构助词，用于引导后置定语。在现代汉语中，定语一般放在被修饰对象前面，但古文可以用"之"引导后置定语。这里的"之"只起到引导后置定语的作用，没有实质意义，可以省译。

3.2.2　省译文化背景

　　英译文言文时，译者也可以省译一些次要的文化背景信息，因为这些信息对译文读者来说属于非必要关注信息。省译不仅没有"损意"，而且可以使译文更加简洁，信息更加聚焦。

译例13 兖州徂徕山寺曰光化，客有习儒业者，坚志栖焉。《太平广记·光化寺客》

汉译 兖州徂徕山上有一个叫光化寺的寺庙，有一个儒生住在里面刻苦学习。

英译 Far away from worldly hustle and bustle, up on Culai Mountain was a Buddhist temple named Guanghua. Once, a young man of the Confucian school took up residence there to concentrate on his books, brushing up for the imperial examinations.（张光前 译）

分析 地名"兖州"在译文中没有出现，因为对译文读者来说，徂徕山和光化寺才是重要的地点信息。此处"兖州"较"徂徕山"而言，是一个更大的地域范围，属于次要背景信息，可以省去不译，省译后的译文对故事的描述更为聚焦，更能传递读者一些有效信息。

3.3　合译

　　古文句子（包括分句、从句、主句）一般偏短，英译时，根据句意关系，可以灵活对一些句子进行合并翻译，从而实现结构紧凑、表达简洁以及语言地道。句子合译有三种常见情形：

　　①英语是形合的语言，用连词将句子连接起来；

　　②将句子作为定语或状语处理，合并到另一个句子；

　　③一些从句，如条件句，有时可以转化成介词短语、定语或其他成分，合并到另一个句子。

译例14 永州之野产异蛇，黑质而白章；触草木，尽死；以啮人，无御之者。然得而腊之以为饵，可以已大风、挛踠、瘘疠，去死肌，杀三虫。其始太医以王命聚之，岁赋其二。募有能捕之者，当其租入。永之人争奔走焉。《捕蛇者说》

汉译 永州的野外出产一种奇特的蛇，它有着黑色的底子和白色的花纹。如果这种蛇碰到草木，草木全都会死；如果被蛇咬到，没有谁能抵挡这种蛇毒。然而捉到后晾干把它做成药饵，可以用来治愈大风、挛踠、瘘、疠，去除死肉，杀死人体内的寄生虫。起初，太医以皇帝的命令征集这种蛇，每年征收两次，招募能够捕捉这种蛇的人，充抵他的赋税。永州的人都争相去捕这种蛇。

英译 ① There is a kind of strange snake in the wilderness of Yongzhou City. It has black skin and white stripes. If it touches a plant, the plant will die and if it bites someone, he can't survive. However, if it is caught, dehydrated and then made into an ingredient of medicine, it can cure leprosy, arthritis, swollen necks, malignant tumors, remove decayed flesh, and eliminate internal parasites that may cause illness. Since early times the court physician has ordered the people in the name of the emperor to hand in the snakes twice a year. If one can be designated to catch the snakes, he will be free of tax. So people in Yongzhou vie with one another to catch the snakes.

② In the wilderness on the outskirts of Yongzhou City lives a kind of snake with black skin and white stripes. Any plant dies upon its touch and anyone bitten by it is doomed to die. But once it is caught and dehydrated, it can serve as an ingredient of a traditional medicine for the cure of leprosy, arthritis, swollen necks, malignant tumors, the removal of decayed flesh, and the elimination of internal parasites that may cause illness. Since early times the court physician has ordered local people in the name of the emperor to hand in the snakes twice a year. Whoever does so is exempted from taxation. People in Yongzhou are vying with one another to catch the snakes.

分析 "黑质而白章"说明蛇的特点。译文②将其灵活转化成定语，用 with 引导介词短语作后置定语，放在前句 snake 的后面，对其进行说明。两句合译成一句，结构更加紧凑。译文①则单独成句，没有对两句进行合译。

"触草木"是一个条件句，意为"如果蛇接触到草木"。译文②利用英语的名词和介词优势，将其转化为介词短语 upon its touch。译文①直译，用 If 引导条件句，表达也对，但没有译文②简洁。

"触草木，尽死；以啮人，无御之者。"分别讲述草木和人接触蛇的后果。语义紧密，可以用 and 连接两个并列句。两个译文均用 and 连接并列结构。

"以啮人"也是条件句，意为"假设蛇用牙齿咬人"。译文②将其转化成分词短语 bitten by it，作后置定语，置于被修饰对象 anyone 的后面。译文①直译，用 If 引导条件句，表达也对，但没有译文②简洁、紧凑。

"然得而腊之以为饵，可以已大风、挛踠、瘘疠，去死肌，杀三虫。"句间存在条件关系。两个译文分别用 if 和 once 连接主从句。

"岁赋其二"中的"赋"和前句的"聚"其实同义，都表示"征收"的意思，故译一个即可，可译为 hand in。句中"岁……二"可以转化成状语 twice a year，直接跟在前句的后面，修饰前面的动作 hand in。两个译文均将其转化成状语，没有单独成句。

关于"募有能捕之者，当其租入"的翻译，在句意不变的前提下，可以像译文①一样，将其转化成 If 引导的主从句结构；也可以像译文②一样，将前一句转化为 whoever 引导的主语从句，再把后一句作为表语连在一起。

两个译文均准确地传达了原文的意思，但译文②使用合译更多，更简洁，效果更好。

真题译·注·评

刘氏子妻

刘氏子者，少任侠，有胆气，常客游楚州淮阴县，交游多市井恶少。邻人王氏有女，求聘之，王氏不许。// 后数岁，因饥。遂从戎。数年后，役罢，再游楚乡。与旧友相遇，甚欢，常恣游骋。昼事弋猎，夕会狭邪。// 因出郭十余里，见一坏墓，棺柩暴露。归而合饮酒。时将夏夜，暴雨初至，众人戏曰："谁能以物送至坏冢棺上者？"刘秉酒恃气曰："我能之。"众曰："若审能之，明日，众置一筵，以赏其事。"乃取一砖，同会人列名于上，令生持去，余人饮而待之。// 生独行，夜半至墓。月初上，如有物蹲踞棺上，谛视之，乃一死妇人也。生舍砖于棺，背负此尸而归。// 众方欢语，忽闻生推门，如负重之声。门开，直入灯前，置尸于地，卓然而立，面施粉黛，鬓发半披。一座绝倒，亦有奔走藏伏者。生曰："此我妻也。"遂拥尸至床同寝。众人惊惧。// 至四更，忽觉口鼻微微有气。诊视之，即已苏矣。问所以，乃王氏之女，因暴疾亡，不知何由至此。未明，生取水，与之洗面濯手，整钗鬓，疾已平复。// 乃闻邻里相谓曰："王氏女将嫁暴卒，未殓，昨夜因雷，遂失其尸。// 生乃以告王氏，王氏悲喜，乃嫁生焉。// 众咸叹其冥契，亦伏生之不惧也。

（选自《太平广记》）

◆◆◆ 译文对照 ◆◆◆

[1]The Corpse on the Coffin

①刘氏子者，少任侠，有胆气，常客游[2]楚州淮阴县，交游多市井恶少。邻人王氏有女，求聘之，王氏不许。

汉译 有个姓刘的小伙子，好侠义之事，极有胆量和勇气，经常在楚州淮阴县游历，结交的朋友多是一些市井无赖。邻居王氏有个女儿，刘生前去求婚，被王家拒绝。

英译 The young son of the Lius was a daring tough who had spent most of his adulthood in Huaiyin County [3]associating with the town thugs. [4]Once, he took a fancy to the daughter of the Wangs, his next-door neighbor. But when he asked for her hand, he was flatly turned down.

1　英文标题一般开门见山，突出主题内容。另外，可以把标题设置得更有趣味性，从而吸引读者。The Corpse on the Coffin 既反映了本文主题，又极具趣味性，有助于吸引读者注意。

2　这里的"楚州"不是读者关注的重点，可以省译。此外，其后还有一个地点"淮阴"，因此可以省译"楚州"，保留县名即可，不影响原文有效信息的传递。

3　associate with sb. 具有贬义，指和不好的人交往。翻译时，注意选词的褒贬色彩，尽量和原文保持一致。

4　Once, he took a fancy to the daughter of the Wangs, his next-door neighbor. But when he asked for her hand, he was flatly turned down。英语不喜欢主语多，也不喜欢主语不断变化。本译文中，三个主语（he）保持一致，有助于信息的连贯和阅读焦点的一致。

②后数岁，因饥。遂从戎。数年后，役罢，再游楚乡。与旧友相遇，甚欢，⁵常恣游骋。昼事弋猎，夕会狭邪。

汉译　几年后，出现饥荒，为了活命，被迫参军。又过了几年，服役结束，再次重返楚州，碰到之前的朋友，十分开心。经常和他们一起恣意游玩，白天一起打猎，晚上就饮酒狂欢。

英译　Things went uneventfully for a few years. Then ⁶a famine struck the land, forcing him to enlist in the army in order to get daily rations. When he was demobilized several years later, he returned to Huaiyin County to seek out his old pals. Together, they roamed the country, hunting during the day and carousing through the night.

③因出郭十余里，见一坏墓，棺柩暴露。归而合饮酒。时将夏夜，暴雨初至，众人戏曰："谁能以物送至坏冢棺上者？"

汉译　有次出城外大概十几里远，看到一个损坏的墓地，棺材都暴露在外面。回来又聚在一起喝酒。当时正是夏天夜晚，刚刚下过一场暴雨。喝酒的时候，有人开玩笑地问道："有谁敢把东西放到白天见到的那具棺材上吗？"

英译　⁷It was a warm summer night and a storm had just rolled past. As the gang sat drinking, someone casually suggested a bet on anyone who dared to go at that late hour to the nameless grave which they had come across during the day's hunting. It was a dilapidated tomb three or four miles out of town and part of the coffin was exposed.

④刘秉酒恃气曰："我能之。"众曰："若审能之，明日，众置一筵，以赏其事。"乃取一砖，同会人列名于上，令生持去，余人饮而待之。

汉译　刘生借着酒劲，说"我敢去"。众人说"如果你能做到，明天摆上一桌宴席，作为奖励"。说完，便取来一块砖，参加酒会的所有人都把名字写在上面，叫刘生拿去放在棺材上，众人则继续喝着酒等他。

英译　Emboldened by wine, Liu offered to go. The gang hoorayed and promised to throw a banquet in his honor if he had the guts to do it. To prove his accomplishment, he had to place a brick on the coffin, on which each of them carved his name. Liu strode out into the night as the group went on with their drinking.

5　"恣"意为"放纵，没有拘束"；"游骋"意为"游玩"；"昼事弋猎，夕会狭邪"意为"白天打猎，晚上饮酒狂欢"。

6　乱世当兵（a famine struck the land, forcing him to enlist in the army）很多都是为了获取口粮能继续活下去。增译"in order to get daily rations"补充说明其目的，凸显乱世当兵的迫不得已。

7　时将夏夜，暴雨初至。只要衔接通顺，译文可以提前。

⑤生独行，夜半至墓。月初上，如有物蹲踞棺上，⁸谛视之，乃一死妇人也。生舍砖于棺，背负此尸而归。

汉译 刘生独自一人上路，半夜才到达坟墓处。月亮刚升上来，朦胧间好像有什么东西蹲在棺材上。刘生仔细查看，原来是个死去的女人。刘生把砖头丢在棺材盖上，背起女尸就回去了。

英译 It was near midnight when he reached the tomb. The moon had just risen over the horizon, revealing the silhouette of a figure crouching on the coffin. He rubbed his eyes and looked again. It was a woman corpse. He slapped the brick on the coffin lid, picked up the body, and carried it on his back.

⑥众方欢语，忽闻生推门，如负重之声。门开，直入灯前，置尸于地，卓然而立，面施粉黛，髻发半披。一座绝倒，亦有奔走藏伏者。生曰："此我妻也。"遂拥尸至床同寝。众人惊惧。

汉译 众人正在欢声笑语，忽然听到刘生推门，好像背着很重的东西。推开门后，刘生直接走到灯前，把女尸放下来，女尸直挺挺地站在地上，脸上还留着粉妆，披头散发。满座的人都被吓到了，还有奔跑着躲藏起来的。刘生说："这就是我的老婆了"。于是把女尸抱上床同寝，其他人都惊呆了。

英译 The gang was still in a noisy revel when they heard a heavy thump against the door. The door flew open and Liu came straight into the lamplight and stood the corpse upright. There she stood, her face powdered pale and her hair hanging loose. The throng was stunned, and some even dashed for cover. "She shall be my wife," Liu announced as he carried the corpse over to the bed and lay down beside it. The mob was glued to the ground.

⑦至⁹四更，忽觉口鼻微微有气。诊视之，即已苏矣。问所以，乃王氏之女，因暴疾亡，不知何由至此。未明，生取水，与之洗面濯手，整钗髻，疾已平复。

汉译 到四更天时，忽然发现女尸口鼻中有轻微的呼吸。仔细一看，女尸已经醒来了。问她怎么回事，原来她就是之前想娶的王家女儿，突发疾病身亡，也不知自己怎么就到了这里。当时天还没亮，刘生拿水给她洗脸洗手，梳洗打扮。王氏的病也已经好了。

英译 When the cock crowed, Liu found that the corpse was breathing faintly. Taking her pulse, he realized that she was coming to. Soon she was able to talk and he learned that she was none other than the daughter of the Wangs. She seemed confused to find herself in such company. For all she remembered, she died of a sudden attack of illness. Liu fetched water to wash her face and helped her make up her hair. Soon after she was fully recovered.

---

8 "谛"为"仔细（听或看）"的意思。

9 "四更"是中国古代的一种时间划分方式，时间范围为凌晨一点至三点。英文中没有对应的表达方式，无法直译，可以采用解释的方式，译为：When the cock crowed（鸡鸣时）。

⑧乃闻邻里相谓曰："王氏女将嫁暴卒，未殓，昨夜因雷，遂失其尸。

汉译 很快，街道邻居都在谈论这件事情，说"王家女儿在出嫁前夕暴病身亡，尸体还没有入殓，昨天夜里突然打雷下雨，尸体转眼便不见了。"

英译 [10]It was now broad daylight outside. People in the streets were excitedly talking about the missing corpse of Wang's daughter, who had died of a sudden illness on the verge of her marriage. The corpse, laid out on the bier for final services, was lost during last night's thunderstorm.

⑨生乃以告王氏，王氏悲喜，乃嫁生焉。

汉译 刘生就将这件事告诉王家人，王家人又悲又喜，就把女儿嫁给了刘生。

英译 Liu went over to tell the Wangs about what had happened. The news swept away their sorrows and they ungrudgingly allowed him to marry their daughter.

⑩众咸叹其冥契，亦伏生之不惧也。

汉译 众人都感叹两人命中注定该成夫妻，也佩服刘生的胆量。

英译 If that was not a predestined marriage bond, it must have been a reward for his bravery.（张光前 译）

◆◆◆ 知识点评 ◆◆◆

（1）分段翻译

原文只有一段，如果译文也只有一段，则显得冗长，影响阅读效果。本文讲述了一个故事，可以根据故事发展的时间顺序分段。以译文前三段作为例：

译例 1 ①刘氏子者，少任侠，有胆气，常客游楚州淮阴县，交游多市井恶少。邻人王氏有女，求聘之，王氏不许。

译文 The young son of the Lius was a daring tough who had spent most of his adulthood in Huaiyin County associating...

②后数岁，因饥。遂从戎。数年后，役罢，再游楚乡。与旧友相遇，甚欢，常恣游骋。昼事弋猎，夕会狭邪。

译文 Things went uneventfully for a few years. Then a famine...

③因出郭十余里，见一坏墓，棺柩暴露。归而合饮酒。时将夏夜，暴雨初至，众人戏曰："谁能以物送至坏冢棺上者？"

10　增译 "It was now broad daylight outside."，有助于内容的衔接。

译文　It was a warm summer night and a storm had just rolled past. As the gang...

分析　第①段对少年时期的刘氏男子做一个介绍，第②段以"后数岁"开头，讲述几年后的事情，和前面一段有明显的时间间隔。第③段讲述他们的一次具体经历，将时间背景"时将夏夜"提前。时间上三处属于较为明显的时间节点，可以独立成段翻译。

另外，故事描述视角或描述对象发生变化时，也可以分段翻译。

译例 2　⑤生独行，夜半至墓。月初上，如有物蹲踞棺上，谛视之，乃一死妇人也。生舍砖于棺，背负此尸而归。

译文　Liu strode out into the night... It was near midnight when he reached...

⑥众方欢语，忽闻生推门，如负重之声。门开，直入灯前，置尸于地，卓然而立，面施粉黛，鬌发半披。一座绝倒，亦有奔走藏伏者。生曰："此我妻也。"遂拥尸至床同寝。众人惊惧。

译文　The gang was still in a noisy revel when they heard a heavy...

分析　第⑤段对刘氏男子进行描述，第⑥段视角转换到他的一伙朋友，可以分段翻译。这样，故事脉络更加清晰，内容更加清楚，便于读者阅读。

（2）语序调整

翻译时可以根据译文表达需要对原文某些句子的先后顺序进行调整，从而使译文衔接更加顺畅。

译例 3　③因出郭十余里，见一坏墓，棺柩暴露。归而合饮酒。时将夏夜，暴雨初至，众人戏曰："谁能以物送至坏冢棺上者？"

译文　It was a warm summer night and a storm had just rolled past. As the gang sat drinking, someone casually suggested...

分析　英语叙事往往先交代背景。"时将夏夜，暴雨初至"属于事件的背景信息，置于段首翻译使故事的展开显得更加自然，更易理解。

（3）灵活增译

原文讲述的是一个故事，英译这个故事需要内容传递完整、衔接顺畅。对比原文和译文可以发现，译文有些地方进行了增译。增译的目的是使译文衔接更加顺畅，故事可读性更强。

译例 4　①刘氏子者，少任侠，有胆气，常客游楚州淮阴县，交游多市井恶少。邻人王氏有女，求聘之，王氏不许。

译文　The young son of the Lius was a daring tough who had spent most of his adulthood in Huaiyin County associating with the town thugs...

②后数岁，因饥。遂从戎。数年后，役罢，再游楚乡。与旧友相遇，甚欢，常恣游骋。昼事弋猎，夕会狭邪。

译文　Things went uneventfully for a few years. Then a famine struck the land...

分析　下划线部分是增译，"之后几年都太平无事"有助于引出后面"突然出现饥荒"，使故事描述更顺畅。如果直接表达"Then a famine struck the land..."，和前面段落结尾衔接有点突兀，不够顺畅，影响译文的可读性。

译例 5　⑦至四更，忽觉口鼻微微有气。诊视之，即已苏矣。问所以，乃王氏之女，因暴疾亡，不知何由至此。未明，生取水，与之洗面濯手，整钗髻，疾已平复。

译文　When the cock crowed, Liu found…. Soon after she was fully recovered.

⑧乃闻邻里相谓曰："王氏女将嫁暴卒，未殓，昨夜因雷，遂失其尸。

译文　It was now broad daylight outside. People in the streets...

分析　下划线部分也是增译的信息。首先，译文按照时间先后顺序分段，增译 "It was now broad daylight outside."，有助于译文分段；其次，此处增译，可以和前一段的 "When the cock crowed" 对应，故事发展脉络更加清晰，读起来也更加通顺。

第 11 讲 非文学翻译

第 1 节 非文学作品特点

1.1 准确规范

　　非文学作品内容广泛，涉及政治、法律、经济、科技等社会生活的各个领域。非文学作品的首要特点是准确。该类作品的主要目的是传递信息，即"说的是什么"，因此信息的准确性非常重要。一旦表达有误，可能会造成严重后果。例如，合同有误可能会引起诉讼和造成金钱损失，医药文本错误可能威胁生命健康。因此，非文学作品的内容要确保准确无误。

　　在内容准确的基础上，非文学作品还要求表达规范。首先，语言表述要规范，用词准确、搭配合理，句子结构符合语法规则，意义明确，没有歧义。其次，专业术语要规范，以确保文本的专业性、准确性和可读性。最后，相关的书写格式要规范。例如，商务信函对格式有严格要求，一旦格式有误，文本会显得不正式、不权威，影响交际效果。

1.2 客观简洁

　　非文学作品和文学作品都是对客观世界的描述。文学作品的描述往往源于生活而又高于生活，允许一定程度的虚构、夸大，以满足一定的艺术需求。而非文学作品多以描述事物、传递信息、说明论述为主，其内容应该真实客观，且条理清楚、逻辑严谨。事件的时间、地点、人物、原因、经过、结果必须真实，事物的外形、大小、性质、特征、用途必须准确，所举的数字、图表、例子必须可靠，一切都应具有客观实在性。

　　文学作品的功能是通过语言文字形象地反映生活，表达作者对人生、社会的认识和感悟，给读者带来艺术的享受。不同于文学作品，非文学作品注重实用性和功能性。有效地给读者传递信息、知识或观点是非文学作品的首要要求，所以表达应尽量做到言简意赅，尽量用朴实的语言，以提高读者的阅读效率。总而言之，非文学作品的表达应直截了当、避免啰嗦、不说废话、不绕圈子。

第 2 节　非文学翻译要点

非文学作品的特点是准确规范、客观简洁，所以对应的译文也要具备以上两个特点。非文学翻译过程中，要注意术语的规范、表达的简洁以及逻辑的严谨。

2.1　术语约定俗成

术语，即"专门学科的专门用语"，其翻译要遵从"约定俗成"和"官方权威"的原则。以政论类文本为例。该类文本经常会出现一些常用术语或习惯性表达，如"中国特色社会主义""科学发展观""新常态"等。此类翻译不可随意发挥，要以官方表达或习惯性表达为准。

译例 1　中国共产党第十七次全国代表大会，是在我国改革发展关键阶段召开的一次十分重要的大会。大会的主题是：高举中国特色社会主义伟大旗帜，以邓小平理论和"三个代表"重要思想为指导，深入贯彻落实科学发展观，继续解放思想，坚持改革开放，推动科学发展，促进社会和谐，为夺取全面建设小康社会新胜利而奋斗。

译文　The Seventeenth Congress is one of vital importance being held at a crucial stage of China's reform and development. The theme of the congress is to hold high the great banner of socialism with Chinese characteristics, follow the guidance of Deng Xiaoping Theory and the important thought of Three Represents, thoroughly apply the Scientific Outlook on Development, continue to emancipate the mind, persist in reform and opening up, pursue development in a scientific way, promote social harmony, and strive for new victories in building a moderately prosperous society in all respects.（十七大官方译文）

分析　以上画横线的表达均为官方译文，其每一个用词都有考究，在翻译时不能随意更改。例如，"中国特色主义"是指中国特有的文化、社会、政治、经济、科技、教育等各个方面的特色，是中国特有的发展模式和实践。它强调了中国的历史文化、社会现状和经济发展状况，以及中国独特的政治、社会和文化价值观。characteristic 是用来描述事物的本质、内在特点或者长期存在的特征，符合"中国特色主义"想要表达的内涵。总之，对于专业术语的翻译，用词必须准确，否则影响译文的专业性、权威性和正式性。

2.2　表述言简意赅

前面【第 1 节】中有讲到非文学作品的特征之一便是"客观简洁"，故其翻译也应尽量做到言简意赅，从而与原文的风格保持一致。

译例 2　树立全民环保意识

译文　① help the whole nation see the importance of environmental protection

② make everybody environmentally aware

译例 3 政务公开
译文 ① make government affairs known to the public
② government transparency

译例 4 完善公开办事制度
译文 ① improve the system of keeping the public informed of matters being handled
② improve the system of public office transparency

译例 5 正确处理改革、发展和稳定的关系
译文 ① properly handle the relation between reform, development and stability
② balance reform, development and stability

译例 6 收入分配关系尚未理顺。
译文 ① Things have yet to be straightened out in the matter of income distribution.
② Income distribution has yet to be rationalized.

分析 上述例子的两个译文虽都无误，但译文②更加简洁、地道、效果更好。其实，有时跳脱字面意思，翻译字面背后的内涵，译文可能比字对字翻译更为精简凝练。比如，译例 5 中，"正确处理改革、发展和稳定的关系"就是"平衡改革、发展和稳定"的意思，直接用 balance 一词便传达出了"正确处理……关系"这一短语的内涵，语言简练。

译例 7 江阴在 2006 年 6 月江阴市第十次党代会上确立了"五民五好"的目标愿景（即：以民生为本，力求个个都有好工作；以民富为纲，力求家家都有好收入；以民享为先，力求处处都有好环境；以民安为基，力求天天都有好心情；以民强为重，力求人人都有好身体。）

译文 ① In June 2006, at the 11th Jiangyin Party Congress, we set the vision of "Five Tenets for the People and Five Goods", which means to provide livelihoods for the people and give them good jobs; create wealth for the people and give them good income; bring bliss for the people and give them a good environment; bring peace for the people and give them good spirits; build strength for the people and give them good health.
② At the 11th Jiangyin Party Congress in June 2006, we set five objectives (the *wuhao* objectives) for government, namely working to provide "good jobs, good income, good environment, good public order and good health" for people.

分析 译文①也算得上准确、通顺，但存在语义的重复表达，略显冗长。仔细分析下原文内容："民生"意指"工作好"；"民富"意指"收入好"；"民享""好环境"；"民安"，则人们"心情好"；"民强"，则人们"身体好"。译文②抓住原文内涵，省译了暗含的重复信息，译文非常精炼，表达效果相对来说更好。

　　要做到表达的简洁，还要避免滥用修饰语，尤其在政论类文本中，很多修饰语没有实质意义，可以省译。

译例 8 坚持弘扬和培育民族精神，切实加强思想道德建设，大力发展教育和科学事业，积极推进文化创新，不断增强中国特色社会主义的吸引力和感召力。

译文 We should continue to carry forward and cultivate the national spirit, promote ideological and ethical progress, develop education and science, make cultural innovation and enhance the attraction and appeal of socialism with Chinese characteristics.

分析 原文中画横线的副词均没有实质意义，从语义角度来看，属于多余的修饰语。例如，"积极推进文化创新"，"推进"肯定是积极的，没有必要再强调"积极"。如果以上副词都翻译出来，译文会冗长拖沓，不地道。

2.3　逻辑严谨无误

非文学作品的功能（传递信息、描述事实、说明论述等）要求其表述逻辑一定要严谨。因此，在翻译非文学作品时，应参考对应学科术语和专业知识，理清背后的逻辑，从而确保译文同原文一样——语言表述正确、逻辑严谨。尤其是当原文字面意思不够具体的时候，更需要深挖字后内涵，从而呈现其内在表述逻辑。

译例 9 我们将突破制约经济社会发展的关键技术。

译文 ① We will make breakthroughs in key technologies that constrain our socioeconomic development.
② We will make breakthroughs in key technologies vital to our socioeconomic development.

分析 怎么会有"制约"而不是"促进"经济发展的关键技术？译文①虽与原文一一对应，实际上却歪曲了原文的意思。原文的"制约"指的是因为缺少这些关键技术，经济社会发展受到制约，因此我们要实现突破。译文②正确理解了原文意思，译为：key technologies vital to our socioeconomic development，将"关键技术"和"经济社会发展"之间真正的关系译出。

译例10 十八大以来，高层领导一再阐明大力推进改革的坚定态度，不断释放锐意改革的清晰信号。（厦门大学·真题）

译文 ① Since the 18th CPC National Congress, senior leaders have repeatedly stressed their firmness in reform and sent out messages on many occasions of accelerating and deepening the reform.
② Since the 18th CPC National Congress, the central government leaders have repeatedly stressed their firmness in reform and sent out messages on many occasions of accelerating and deepening the reform.

分析 原文中"高层领导"表意模糊，译文①直译为 senior leaders，读者可能会感到困惑，到底是哪个级别的高层领导？县级、市级、省级还是中央级？根据后文"一再阐明大力推进改革的坚定态度，不断释放锐意改革的清晰信号"推断，这里的"高层领导"指的应是中央政府领导，因此可以译为 the central government leaders，参考译文②。

译例11 要把改革的力度、发展的速度和社会可承受的程度统一起来。

译文 ① Integrate the momentum of reform and the speed of development with the resilience of the general public.
② Balance the momentum of reform and the speed of development against the resilience of the general public.

分析 原文意思是改革力度和发展速度要考虑社会可承受的程度。改革力度太大、发展速度太快可能会超出社会可承受的限度。译文②正确传达了原文的意思。译文①将"把……统一起来"直译为 integrate...with，字面意思看似一致，但 integrate 表达的是"（使）合并，成为一体"的意思。读者可能会困惑，这三者怎么能结合为一个整体？译文①既没有理解原文意思，也没有掌握 integrate 的用法。

译例12 鼓励社会力量办学。

译文 ① Encourage social forces to run schools.

② Encourage non-governmental sectors to run schools.

分析 中国一直以来大多都是政府投资办学，因此办学力量一般是政府机构。鼓励"社会力量"办学，实则是指鼓励"非政府机构"办学。译文①中的 social forces 指社会制度、文化、价值观、经济、政治等影响和塑造社会发展和变革的各种因素和力量，范围过大，不够具体化。翻译时，应根据原文内涵，将"社会力量"具体译为"非政府机构"，即 non-governmental sectors。译文②理解到位，译文更贴切。

真题译·注·评

◆◆◆ **译文对照** ◆◆◆

发展更加公平更高质量的教育。构建德智体[1]美劳全面培养的教育体系。推动义务教育优质均衡发展和城乡一体化，加快[2]补齐农村办学条件短板，健全教师工资保障长效机制，改善乡村教师待遇。进一步提高学前教育入园率，完善普惠性学前教育保障机制，支持社会力量办园。[3]鼓励高中阶段学校多样化发展，加强县域高中建设。增强职业教育适应性，深化产教融合、校企合作，[4]深入实施职业技能等级证书制度。（中国科学技术大学·真题）

We will develop more equitable and higher-quality education. We will build an education system that ensures the well-rounded development of students in terms of moral grounding, intellectual and physical ability, aesthetic sensibility, and work skills. We will promote high-quality, well-balanced, and integrated development of compulsory education in both urban and rural areas. We will work quickly to improve the basic conditions of rural schools, refine the long-term mechanism for ensuring salary payments to teachers, and improve the pay packages of teachers in rural schools. We will raise the preschool enrollment rate, improve the mechanism to support public-interest pre-school education, and support private actors in running kindergartens. We will encourage the diversified development of senior secondary schools and the development of county high schools. We will enhance the adaptability of vocational education, deepen industry-education integration and school-enterprise cooperation, and implement the system of vocational technical grade certificates.

办好特殊教育、继续教育，支持和规范民办教育发展。[5]分类建设一流大学和一流学科，加快优化学科专业结构，[6]加强基础学科和前沿学科建设，促进新兴交叉学科发展。支持中西部高等教育发展。加大国家通用语言文字推广力度。发挥在线教育优势，完善终身学习体系。倡导全社会尊师重教。深化教育评价改革，健全学校家庭社会协同育人机制，规范校外培训。加强师德师

1　这里的"美"指的是审美能力，可以译为 aesthetic sensibility。

2　"补齐短板"是汉语中的文化特色词，表达非常形象，直译成英文无法传递其内涵。因此，译文采取意译方式，译为 improve the basic conditions。

3　"鼓励高中阶段学校多样化发展"和"加强县域高中建设"可以合译，共用谓语动词encourage，从而使译文更简洁。

4　"深入"属于多余的副词修饰，没有实际意义，可以省译。

5　"分类建设一流大学和一流学科"指的是在分类的基础上建设，比如，大学分为双一流A类和B类。译文on a categorized basis 准确地传达了原文的意思。

6　"加强基础学科和前沿学科建设"和"促进新兴交叉学科发展"可以合译，共用谓语动词 promote。

风建设。在教育公平上迈出更大步伐，更好解决进城务工人员子女就学问题，高校招生继续 [7] 加大对中西部和农村地区倾斜力度，努力让广大学生健康快乐成长，让每个孩子都有人生出彩的机会。

We will provide high-quality special education and continuing education, and support the development of private schools in a well-regulated way. We will develop first-rate universities and academic disciplines on a categorized basis, move faster to improve the composition of disciplines and majors, and promote the development of foundational disciplines, cutting-edge disciplines, and emerging inter-disciplinary fields. We will support the development of higher education in the central and western regions. Efforts to promote standard spoken and written Chinese will be stepped up. We will give full play to the advantages of online education, improve the lifelong learning system, and encourage public respect for teachers and public support for education. We will further the reform of educational assessment, improve the mechanism of school-family-society cooperation in educating students, and keep off-campus training well-regulated. We will strengthen the professional ethics and [8] competence of teachers, and make major strides in ensuring equitable education. We will endeavor to provide better schooling for children of rural migrant workers in cities, and continue to have universities and colleges enroll more students from the central and western regions and rural areas. We will ensure that students live healthy and happy lives and that every child has the opportunity to make their life shine brilliantly.

◆◆◆ 知识点评 ◆◆◆

（1）后置定语的翻译

英语前置定语不能太长。当汉语定语偏长，翻译时定语往往需要后置，放在被修饰对象的后面。总的来说，英译后置定语可以灵活采用五种处理方式，将其译为：定语从句、分词短语、形容词短语、介词短语和动词不定式。

译例 1 构建德智体美劳全面培养的教育体系。

译文 We will build an education system that ensures the well-rounded development of students in terms of moral grounding, intellectual and physical ability, aesthetic sensibility, and work skills.

译例 2 健全教师工资保障长效机制

译文 refine the long-term mechanism for ensuring salary payments to teachers

译例 3 完善普惠性学前教育保障机制

译文 improve the mechanism to support public-interest pre-school education

---

7 "加大倾斜力度"是一种形象说法，直译成英语无法传递其内涵，可以采用意译，解释它的意思，即招收更多来自中西部地区的学生。

8 "加强师德师风建设"指教师不仅要有好的职业道德，还要提升自身能力。因此，译文增译了 strengthen...competence of teachers，使逻辑更加严谨。

译例 4　**加大国家通用语言文字推广力度。**

译文　Efforts to promote standard spoken and written Chinese will be stepped up.

分析　原文画横线处定语偏长，翻译时均不能前置，因此采用定语从句、介词短语和动词不定式的方式将其后置。需要指出的是，同一个句子里面后置定语可以有多个选择。比如，译例 2 中的定语"教师工资保障"可以翻译为 for ensuring salary payments to teachers，也可以译为 to ensure salary payments to teachers 或 that ensures salary payments to teachers。

(2) 复合词的使用

英语复合词通常由两个或两个以上自由词素构成，表达单一的语义概念。复合词的组成部分有时连在一起写，有时用连字符 "-" 连起来。汉英翻译中，复合词的使用可以使句子结构更加简单，表达更加简洁。

译例 5　**增强职业教育适应性，深化产教融合、校企合作，深入实施职业技能等级证书制度。**

译文　We will enhance the adaptability of vocational education, deepen industry-education integration and school-enterprise cooperation, and implement the system of vocational technical grade certificates.

译例 6　**深化教育评价改革，健全学校家庭社会协同育人机制，规范校外培训。**

译文　We will further the reform of educational assessment, improve the mechanism of school-family-society cooperation in educating students, and keep off-campus training well-regulated.

分析　若不使用复合词，译例 5 中汉语画横线部分可以直译为 deepen the integration of industry into education and increase cooperation between schools and enterprises；译例 6 中汉语画横线部分可以直译为：improve the mechanism where school, family and society can cooperate in educating students，但是与使用复合词的译文相比，后者表达更为简洁，句子更加紧凑，表达效果也更好。

第12讲　汉英翻译常见问题总结

　　翻译分"理解"和"表达"两个过程。学生在这两个过程中，均存在不少问题：有的问题源于语言功底不好，有的源于语言差异，有的源于对翻译存在错误的理解。这些问题其实在前面都讨论过，本讲只是进行一个总结。希望各位读者重视这些问题，后期通过不断的学习以减少错误，使译文更加准确、地道。

　　本讲总结的七大问题分别是：理解错误、用词不当、搭配不当、语法错误、重复啰嗦、文化意识浅以及语言不地道。

第1节　理解错误

　　学生往往低估了汉语理解的难度，只获取字面意义，而汉语表达有时较为含蓄，字面意义并不能传达其语境意义。汉英翻译时，对原文的理解要考虑文章背景、作者背景和上下文语境等多种因素，以避免理解偏颇或理解有误。

译例1　闻名于世的丝绸之路是一系列连接东西方的路线。<u>丝绸之路是古代中国的丝绸贸易</u>。<u>丝绸之路上的贸易在中国、南亚、欧洲发挥了重要作用</u>。

译文　① The world-renowned Silk Road is a series of routes connecting the East to the West. <u>The Silk Road is the ancient Chinese silk trade.</u> The Silk Road trade played an important role in China, South Asia and Europe.

　　② The world-renowned Silk Road is a series of routes connecting the East to the West. The road, <u>opened to deliver silk produced by ancient China</u>, played an important role in promoting trade between China, South Asia and Europe.

分析　"丝绸之路是古代中国的丝绸贸易"这句话语义模糊，且字面逻辑存在问题，因为"路"和"贸易"不能等同。如果像译文①一样，直译为"The Silk Road is the ancient Chinese silk trade."，这样的表达是错误的，而且译文读者也没法理解它的意思。结合历史文化背景可知，丝绸之路是古代中国开辟的一条道路，最初作用是运输中国古代出产的丝绸。因此，可以译为"The road, opened to deliver silk produced by ancient China..."，参考译文②。

译例2　我父亲在剪破的月影下，闻到了比现在强烈无数倍的腥甜气息。那时候，余司令牵着他的手在高粱地里行走，三百多个乡亲叠股枕臂、陈尸狼藉，流出的鲜血灌溉了一大片高粱，把高粱下的黑土浸泡成稀泥，使他们拔脚迟缓。腥甜的气味令人窒息……（扬州大学·真题）

译文　① In the moonlight, my father <u>smelled a strong and sweet smell far stronger than it is now</u>. At that time, Commander Yu held his hand and walked in the sorghum field. The corpses of more than three hundred villagers were scattered on the ground. The blood irrigated a large area of sorghum, soaking the black soil under it into a thin mud, causing them to pull their feet slowly. The pungent and sweet smell was suffocating...

②　General Yu was leading my father by the hand through the sorghum. Suddenly my father got a whiff of a blood odor, far stronger than anything you might smell today. Through the moonlight they saw corpses of more than 300 fellow villagers, piled and scattered on the ground. Their blood soaked the sorghum field and the sticky mud slowed the two down. The blood smell was suffocating...

分析　译文①画横线处有明显的理解错误。首先，对"腥甜气息"的理解有误。根据下文可以得知，这里的"腥甜气息"指人死后散发出来的腥臭味。虽然"甜"是褒义词，但"腥甜"一词却表示贬义，不能译为 sweet，否则不符合语境。此外，"闻到了比现在强烈无数倍的腥甜气息"表述并不完整，译文①直译，不仅存在错译，意思也表述不清楚。该句完整理解应该是：闻到了比现在能够闻到的气息强烈无数倍的腥甜血味。译文②增译为 "...got a whiff of a blood odor, far stronger than anything you might smell today."。同时把"腥甜气息"译为 a blood odor，准确地传达了原文的意思。

第 2 节　用词不当

用词不当指词不达意或词义强弱、情感、言外之意、语域等和原文不符，是学生翻译时存在的一大问题，也是后期学习需要高度重视的问题。学生平时要养成勤查词典的习惯，了解单词的用法和搭配，并大量阅读地道的英语材料，培养好的语感，以实现翻译时恰当用词。

在前面的章节中，我们已经学习过很多有关用词不当的例子。我们再看两个例子：

译例 1　**济南的人们在冬天是面上含笑的**。（老舍《济南的冬天》）

译文　① The people of Jinan would always beam with delight in winter days.

② The people of Jinan seem to smile throughout winter.

分析　译文①中的 beam 属于用词不当。beam 的英语释义为 to smile with obvious pleasure，用在这里有点表意过头。此外，就算用 beam，也不需要加 with delight，因为它的意思已暗含在 beam 中，无需重复表达。译文②中的 smile 意为"微笑"，是淡淡的笑，更符合原文笑的程度。

译例 2　**数千人聚在一起示威游行，抗议这些新提案**。

译文　① Thousands of people gathered to parade, protesting against the new proposals.

② Thousands of people gathered to demonstrate against the new proposals.

分析　parade 和 demonstrate 都有"游行"的意思，但 parade 一般是为了庆祝，而 demonstrate 是为了抗议或表达不满。译文①用词不当，其感情色彩与原文相反。

第 3 节　搭配不当

这里的"搭配"含义较广，既包括习惯性搭配，如 Merry Christmas 和 Happy New Year，也包括主谓搭配、动宾搭配、主表搭配以及修饰语和被修饰语的搭配。不了解单词用法的情况下，仅凭单词字面意义把相关单词组合在一起，便容易出现大量搭配错误。

搭配不当在本书【第 1 讲 第 2 节】中有详细论述，这里举一例做简要分析。

译例　对于一个在北平住惯的人，像我，冬天要是不刮大风，便是奇迹；济南的冬天是没有风声的。对于一个刚由伦敦回来的人，像我，冬天要能看得见日光，便是怪事；济南的冬天是响晴的。自然，在热带的地方，日光是永远那么毒，响亮的天气，反有点叫人害怕。可是，在北中国的冬天，而能有温晴的天气，济南真得算个宝地。（老舍《济南的冬天》）

译文　Calm in winter would be a miracle to a habitual dweller of Beijing like me; here in Jinan there is no wind whistling in winter. Sunlight in winter would be a wonder to a fresh returnee from London like me; here in Jinan it is always sunny in winter. It goes without saying that sunlight is always scorching in tropic zone where bright sunny weather would sound a bit alarming to people like me. But when it comes to winter in north China, blessed with mild sunny weather, Jinan is indeed a precious land.

分析　译文画横线处均属于搭配不当。

① habitual 一般和"行为"或"动作"搭配，如 a habitual thief（惯偷）、habitual drug use（吸毒成瘾）、habitual meanness（一贯的卑劣行为）。"偷"、"吸毒"、"卑劣行为"都带有动作的含义，而 dweller 强调一种身份，即"居民"，不是强调"住"，所以和 habitual 不能搭配。

②说 Sunlight 是 wonder，语义上过于夸大，阳光不至于到惊奇（wonder）那个程度。

③ sunlight 不能和 scorching 搭配，只能说 "Sun is scorching"。

④ weather 本身也不会 alarming，不具备 alarming 的性质或特征，语义不搭配。

搭配不当其实和用词不当是相通的，搭配不当往往就是用词不当导致的。

第 **4** 节　语法错误

语法是翻译的基础，直接影响到译文质量。汉英翻译中，语法问题也是一大问题。若语法基础不扎实，就容易出现大量语法错误。如：

译例 1　首先，新科技使批量生产成为现实，从而促进了手机的普及。

译文　① To begin with, new technologies make mass-production a reality and promote the popularity of mobile phones.

② To begin with, new technologies have made mass-production a reality, allowing the popular use of mobile phones.

分析　时态是英语语法的基石，直接关系到整个句子的意义和上下文的逻辑。分析原文可知，原文强调"新科技"的积极影响，以及这一影响带来的成果。译文①采用一般现在时，仅表示对目前客观事实的陈述，而译文②采用现在完成时，突出了主语"新科技"对现在的影响，这一影响还可能继续持续下去。因此，从语法角度而言，译文②优于译文①。此外，译文①采用"and"连接两个分句，处理为并列关系，而译文②厘清原文内涵，采用现在分词引导结果状语，句子结构更为清晰明了。因此，从逻辑角度而言，译文②更胜一筹。

译例 2　五岁的时候，我爸爸送我去上学。

译文　① At the age of five, my father sent me to school.

② At the age of five, I was sent to school by my father.

分析　译例 2 的汉语原文虽简单，但翻译时却未必能翻对。因为此处涉及到悬垂修饰语这一语法点：短语在句子中作状语时，其逻辑主语（亦称隐含主语）通常应该是整个句子的主语；否则，就会被认为是语言失误。译文①中，短语"At the age of five"的逻辑主语是"my father"，其语义为：我爸爸五岁的时候，送我去上学。显然，这既不符合汉语原文的含义，也不符合常识。将其改为"At the age of five, I was sent to school by my father."或"When I was five, my father sent me to school."，不仅忠实地传达了原文语义，还避免了犯此类语法错误。

第 5 节　重复啰嗦

汉英翻译时，"重复啰嗦"也是一个普遍问题。汉语多重复，而英语少重复，学生在翻译时容易受汉语母语影响，忽视英语的语言特点，译文往往重复啰嗦。

译例　中国人自古以来就在中秋节庆祝丰收，这与北美地区庆祝感恩节的风俗十分相似。过中秋节的习俗于唐代早期在中国各地开始流行。中秋节在农历八月十五，是人们拜月的节日，这天夜晚皓月当空，人们合家团聚，共赏明月。

译文　① Since ancient times, Chinese people usually celebrate harvest on the Mid-Autumn Festival, which is similar to the custom of celebrating Thanksgiving in the North America. The Mid-Autumn Festival became popular all over China in the early Tang dynasty. The Mid-Autumn Festival celebrated on the 15th day of the 8th month of the lunar calendar, is a day for worshiping the moon. On that day, family members get together and enjoy the bright moon in the sky at night.

② Chinese people have been celebrating harvest on the Mid-Autumn Festival ever since ancient days, much the way North Americans celebrate Thanksgiving. The Chinese festival, celebrated on lunar August 15th, came to be popular all over China in early Tang dynasty. It is a day for worshiping the moon. At that night, family members sit together, enjoying the glorious full moon.

分析　相比译文②，译文①重复较多，语言不够简练。Mid-Autumn Festival 连续出现三次，用词单调，不符合英语避免重复的写作习惯。译文②则用了替代（The Chinese festival）和照应（It）的方式进行替换。译文①将"在农历八月十五"译为 on the 15th day of the 8th month of the lunar calendar，意思虽然也对，但表达很啰嗦，可以简化为 on lunar August 15th，参考译文②。最后，译文①中 the bright moon in the sky 也存在重复表达。in the sky 属于不言而明的信息，因为月亮肯定在天上，不需要重复强调。

第 6 节　文化意识浅

　　翻译是一种跨文化的交际活动，要考虑目的语读者对源语相关社会文化背景的理解能力。我们都知道的背景知识，英美国家读者不一定知道。因此，汉英翻译时，译者应增强文化意识，为使目的语读者更好地理解译文，对一些重要的文化背景需要补充相关信息，但对于一些次要的文化背景，则可以省略。

译例　荣昌位于重庆市西部，地处渝西川东结合部，距重庆市区 88.5 公里，距成都市区 246 公里，成渝高速公路、成渝铁路穿境而过。
荣昌历史悠久，自唐肃宗乾元 2 年（公元 759 年）设县至今，已有 1300 多年……

译文　① Rongchang is located in the west of Chongqing Municipality, bordering eastern Sichuan province. It is 88.5 km away from the downtown area of the municipality and 246 km away from the city of Chengdu. It meets Chengdu-Chongqing freeway and Chengdu-Chongqing railway.

Rongchang boasts a long history of more than 1300 years starting from 759 A.D. in Suzong reign of the Tang dynasty...

② Rongchang is a county situated in the west of Chongqing Municipality bordering eastern Sichuan province. It is 88.5 km from the urban area of Chongqing and 246 km from the city of Chengdu, the capital of Sichuan. The place is accessible by the Chongqing-Chengdu freeway and railway running through it.

Rongchang has a long history of more than 1,300 years, dating back to 759 A.D. when the county was first established in the Tang dynasty...（施晓菁 译）

分析　原文是一个旅游文本的片段。旅游文本一般包含大量的地理、历史、文化、社会信息。这些信息对于源语读者来说往往不言而喻，但对英美国家读者来说可能十分陌生。必要时，应予以解释说明。如：荣昌是重庆市下辖的一个县，译文②增译 a county 进行补充说明，以帮助读者更好地了解该地；成都是四川省的省会，英美国家读者不一定清楚，故增译 the capital of Sichuan；"唐肃宗乾元 2 年（公元 759 年）"涉及的历史背景知识，不需要全部翻译（"唐肃宗"和他的年号"乾元"不是译文读者关注的焦点，可不译。就算翻译出来，他们也难以理解，所以只需要传达"唐朝"和"公元 759 年"这两个细节即可）。译文①完全直译原文，没有考虑到文化背景信息的处理（译文①也有表达问题，但本节只分析和文化背景相关的问题）。

第 7 节　语言不地道

　　译文的地道与否更难把握。没有哪个中国人敢说自己的表达是百分之百地道的。我们生活在中国，母语为汉语，很少有机会接触地道英语环境，所以译文或多或少会有一些不地道的地方，但每个人都可以通过不断的学习精进自己的语言运用能力，从而使自己的译文变得更加地道。因此，翻译，尤其是地道的翻译，是一个活到老、学到老的事情。在学好单词、语法、中英文区别，并大量阅读外文材料的基础上，语言的地道程度是可以不断提高的。

译例 1　中国公司想创造世界品牌，外国公司想增加在中国的销量，这些都正改变着中国的设计产业。中国制造商意识到，若他们想在本国市场脱颖而出，在外国市场崭露头角，就必须设计更好的产品。索尼这样的外国公司也开始明白，从前海外公司常把随便什么地方设计的产品拿到中国来卖，而现在，中国消费者变得更加挑剔，他们不再那样容易满足了。

译文　①Chinese companies' wish to create world famous brands and foreign companies' wish to promote sales in China are transforming China's design industry. Chinese manufacturers have realized that in order to stand out in the domestic market and to emerge in the international, they must design better products. Foreign companies like Sony also come to realize Chinese consumers are becoming pickier and it is not easy as before to satisfy them with any designs from anywhere.

②The Chinese world of design is being transformed by the twin desires of Chinese companies seeking to establish brands globally and foreign companies trying to increase their sales within China. Domestic companies have come to realize that they must improve product design to stand out at home, and also to make a name in the international market. Likewise, global companies like Sony now realize that they can no longer sell slapdash, designed-elsewhere products in China, because Chinese consumers nowadays are far more demanding and difficult to please.

分析　译文①基本上符合英语语法规则，也传达了原文的意思，但句子结构存在三个问题：
　　• 中国公司想创造世界品牌，外国公司想增加在中国的销量，这些都正改变着中国的设计产业。
　　译文①直译原文，句子主语太长，显得头重脚轻，表达效果欠佳。译文②使用被动结构，避开了头重脚轻。这里还涉及一个中英文表达顺序的问题：汉语一般先原因再结果；而英语往往先讲结果，再解释原因，尤其是当原因状语偏长的时候。从这一点来看，译文②更符合英语的表达习惯。此外，"...Chinese companies seeking to establish brands globally and foreign companies trying to increase their sales within China." 是一个平行结构，用两个现在分词短语分别对前面的对象进行修饰，句子结构显得对称，读起来更加顺畅。

• 若他们想在本国市场脱颖而出，在外国市场崭露头角

译文①的 in order to stand out in the domestic market and to emerge in the international 放在复合句中宾语从句的开头，显得整个句子结构不协调，应该放在句尾。

• 更加挑剔

译文①中的 pickier 具有贬义（原文没有贬义），而且过于口语化，没有译文②的 far more demanding 正式，不符合原文的语言风格，不够地道。

总的来说，译文②比译文①更为地道。

译例 2 尽管全球大量的电子产品和鞋等都是中国制造，但这些产品的设计都是在欧美或日本完成的。中国公司制造自己品牌的产品时，通常是模仿国外。但如今不同了，他们都想开创自己的品牌。随着中国公司在设计上的改进，跨国公司意识到，他们的产品需要专门针对中国消费者的品味进行"量身定做"了。

译文 ① Although globally a great number of electronic products and footwear are made in China, all their designs are completed in Europe, America and Japan. The Chinese companies usually modeled on products of foreign companies when they produced their own. Now, the situation is different: they all want to develop their own brands. As the Chinese are improving their design, the multinationals realize their products need to be tailored to the taste of Chinese consumers.

② Many electronic goods and shoes sold all over the world are manufactured in China, yet most of them are designed in Europe, the United States and Japan. In the past, when Chinese companies created their own brands, they usually imitated foreign designs. However, the situation is changing. As Chinese designs improve, multinationals now understand that their products must be "tailored" to Chinese consumer needs.

分析 译文①存在三个问题：

• footwear 是不可数名词，不能被 a great number of 修饰。

• 原文第一句话介绍总体情形：大量中国产品的设计都是在欧美或日本完成。第二句话描述过去的情况。第一句和第二句语义并没有明显的承接标志。译文①直译原文，读起来衔接不够顺畅。译文②增译 In the past，译文衔接更加顺畅，同时和后面的"如今"相呼应，逻辑更加清晰。

• 原文"他们都想开创自己的品牌"的意义已经包含在上下文中，不用重复表达。"过去模仿"，"现在不同"，后边又讲到"中国公司在设计方面的改进"，这些都已经暗含了"要开创自己的品牌"。译文①重复翻译，不够简洁。

译文①总体来说没有译文②地道。

从以上译例可以看出，要想翻译地道，不仅要学好单词、语法，还要了解中英文的区别。此外，大量阅读英语外刊或英语文学作品也有助于学习一些地道的英语表达，丰富自己的译文。

真题译·注·评

◆◆◆ **译文对照** ◆◆◆

七天之后，八月十五日，中秋节。一轮明月冉冉升起，遍地高粱肃然默立，高粱穗子浸在月光里，像蘸过水银，汩汩生辉。（扬州大学·真题）

Seven days later, it was lunar August 15th, the Mid-Autumn Festival. A bright moon was climbing slowly in the sky. Thick sorghum and their spikes stood silently in the ground, gleaming in moonlight as if they had been dipped in mercury. [1] It was deadly quiet.

我父亲在 [2] 剪破的月影下，闻到了比现在强烈无数倍的腥甜气息。那时候，余司令牵着他的手在高粱地里行走，三百多个乡亲叠股枕臂、陈尸狼藉，流出的鲜血灌溉了一大片高粱，把高粱下的黑土浸泡成稀泥，使他们拔脚迟缓。

General Yu was leading my father by the hand through the sorghum. Suddenly my father got a whiff of a blood odor, far stronger than anything you might smell today. Through the moonlight they saw corpses of more than 300 fellow villagers, piled and scattered on the ground. Their blood soaked the sorghum field and the sticky mud slowed the two down.

腥甜的气味令人窒息，一群前来吃人肉的狗，坐在高粱地里，目光炯炯地盯着父亲和余司令。余司令掏出自来得手枪，甩手一响，两只狗眼灭了；又一甩手，灭了两只狗眼。群狗一哄而散，坐得远远的，呜呜地咆哮着，贪婪地望着死尸。

The blood smell was suffocating. A pack of corpse-eating dogs were there, staring at General Yu and my father. Yu took out a pistol and shot one dog. *Bang!* A dog fell down. *Bang!* Another was shot to death. The others ran away to a distant ground, growling and greedily staring at the corpses.

[3] 腥甜味愈加强烈，余司令大喊一声："日本狗！狗娘养的日本！"他对着那群狗打完了所有的子弹，狗跑得无影无踪。

1　增译 "It was deadly quiet." 有两个原因：首先，使得段落结尾更加自然；其次，进一步凸显当时那种一点声音都没有，甚至有点恐怖的氛围。

2　"我父亲在剪破的月影下，闻到了比现在强烈无数倍的腥甜气息"中的"剪破的"修饰月影没有任何实质意义，可以省译；"闻到了比现在强烈无数倍的腥甜气息"完整的理解应是：闻到了比现在能够闻到的气息强烈无数倍的腥甜血味。

3　"腥甜味愈加强烈"中的"甜"不能翻，虽然"甜"是褒义词，但"腥甜"一词却表示贬义，原文传达的是难闻的血腥味。

The sickly smell became stronger. "Japs dog! Fuck you Japanese!" yelled Yu. He fired all bullets. The dogs ran away in an instant, completely out of view.

　　余司令对我父亲说："走吧，儿子！"一老一小，便迎着月光，向高粱深处走去。[4] 那股弥漫田野的腥甜味浸透了我父亲的灵魂，在以后更加激烈更加残忍的岁月里，这股腥甜味一直伴随着他。

"Let's go, son." Yu said to my father. They walked into the thick sorghum. The permeating smell that night was imprinted in my father's mind and accompanied him in the following harder and crueler years.

◆◆◆ 知识点评 ◆◆◆

（1）灵活变通

译例1　余司令掏出自来得手枪，甩手一响，两只狗眼灭了；又一甩手，灭了两只狗眼。群狗一哄而散，坐得远远的，呜呜地咆哮着，贪婪地望着死尸。

译文　Yu took out a pistol and shot one dog. *Bang!* A dog fell down. *Bang!* Another was shot to death. The others ran away to a distant ground, growling and greedily staring at the corpses.

分析　翻译不能硬翻，尤其是当目的语找不到对应表达的时候。"甩手一响"英语找不到直接对应的表达，其意义实则是"开了一枪"；"两只狗眼灭了"是"狗死了"的形象化表达，直译传达不出其真正含义，有同学硬译为 two eyes were eliminated，这是行不通的，因为 eyes 和 eliminated 不能搭配，且该翻译表意与原文表意不符。这种情况下，可以在翻译之前思考其内涵，然后将其转化为一个通俗的、同义的表达方式。后面的"又一甩手，灭了两只狗眼"可以用相同方式处理。

原文"两只狗眼"和"灭了"出现两次，就是两条狗被打死的意思，译文分别译为"A dog fell down."和"Another was shot to death."，多元化处理了表意相同的句子。

（2）抓"实"去"虚"

译例2　余司令掏出自来得手枪，甩手一响，两只狗眼灭了……

译文　Yu took out a pistol and shot one dog. *Bang!* A dog fell down...

分析　翻译要去"虚"，即去掉一些非常次要的、没有交际意义的信息。原文"自来得"是一个枪的牌子，属于次要可忽略的信息，读者的关注重心也不在此。直译出来，对读者也没有意义，可以省译。

4　那股弥漫田野的腥甜味浸透了我父亲的灵魂。"浸透灵魂"不能译为 soak soul，因为 soak 不能和 soul 搭配，soak 是"使湿透"的意思，其后一般接实物，而 soul 为虚拟的对象，虚无缥缈，无法作 soak 的宾语。"浸透灵魂"实则意指深深地印刻在某人心里，可以转化译为 "sth. is imprinted in one's mind."。

译例 3　一群前来吃人肉的狗，坐在高粱地里，<u>目光炯炯</u>地盯着父亲和余司令。

译文　A pack of corpse-eating dogs were there, staring at General Yu and my father.

分析　"目光炯炯"指两眼明亮有神，一般是用来修饰人的，而且往往带有褒义。原文用"目光炯炯"来修饰（日本）狗看人的动作，明显没有褒义。若是直译"目光炯炯"，译文读者将无法理解，为什么一群前来吃人肉的狗还用具有褒义的表述？根据上下文可知，原文侧重"盯着看"的动作，"目光炯炯"即使译出对传递原文信息也没有助益，反而有错译的可能，故可以省译。

附一：真题翻译练习 10 篇

◆◆◆ **真题 10 篇** ◆◆◆

① 天津大学

再穷不能穷教育，再难不能不办学。地处南半球地广人稀的澳大利亚从建国之初，就将教育事业放在首位。首创的空中学校，受到世界各国学习的楷模。澳大利亚全国 2170 万人口主要集中在东南部和北部沿海的几个大城市里，在广阔的内陆及边远地区，只住着疏疏落落的一小部分从事牧业、矿业和铁路运输的居民以及土著居民，他们多数居住在远离城镇的地区。因此，一种非常独特的专门为满足由于疾病、伤残或者居住在偏远地区不能像其他儿童那样入校学习的孩子们需要的空中学校便应运而生了。

在我国，战争年代，后方解放区因为战争的需要，曾出现过马背学校，而今的澳大利亚利用现代化手段办起了空中学校，深受当地孩子们的欢迎。澳大利亚大陆是一个公认的后起发达的资本主义国家，不仅仅是经济在短短几十年间就走向世界前列，而且多发明多创造，既是世界有名的环保国家，也是注重教育的国家。发明空中学校，在世界当属首创。

翻译区：_____

_____

_____

_____

_____

_____

_____

_____

_____

_____

_____

_____

_____

_____

_____

_____

② 华中师范大学

他们生活在上海的市民堆里，不免要受影响，积攒些家底，好过长久日子。但主要兴趣还是在吃上面，夫妻俩的工资，主要也是花在吃上面。在奶奶看来，他们的吃，主要是肯花钱，还有食欲旺盛，其实是不大会吃的。比如，他们三天两头地下馆子，所下的馆子不外是那几个。马路对面的复兴西餐社，绿野川扬菜馆，再远些的，就是南京路上的新雅粤菜馆，洪长兴羊肉馆。倒也不是说这些餐馆不好，而是说，他们实在是没有多少辨别力，多是慕名而去，去了便一而再，再而三，吃得又大多是那几个菜，味厚的，量大的。这也是军队里带来的作风，大鱼大肉。

奶奶烧的一手扬州菜，正合了他们的口味；同时，也将他们的口味提高了。在扬州菜的熟、烂、味透、酱色足底下，是精工、细料、慢火。奶奶的扬州菜又是乡间的一路，用料要重些，尤其多用酱油，风格也略微粗放。在他们吃来，就是至味了。因此，他们就经常地在家中开宴，招待朋友。客人们全都为奶奶的手艺倾倒。他们的朋友也多，多少有些行伍气的，豪爽热情，来了就坐，坐下就吃。所以，家中几乎三日一小席，五日一大宴，日子过得轰轰烈烈。

翻译区：_____

_____

_____

_____

_____

_____

_____

_____

_____

_____

_____

_____

_____

_____

_____

_____

3　北京林业大学

目前，石化产业在快速发展中长期积累的矛盾日益凸现。经济发展方式比较粗放，结构性矛盾比较突出，行业经济规模大而不强，资源环境约束加大。去年下半年以来，受国际金融危机影响，石化产业受到严重冲击，迫切需要通过结构调整和产业升级，提高行业整体素质和市场竞争力。

我国石化产品结构性矛盾突出，集中表现在石化产品、有机化工产品和高档新产品的比重过低，高消耗、粗加工、低附加值产品比重偏高。只有通过技术创新，大力发展新产品制备技术和深加工技术，延伸产业链，拓宽产品幅度，实现产品的高性能化、专用化、绿色化和高附加值化，才能优化产品的结构，提高产业的竞争力和为国民经济相关产业的配套能力。

翻译区：

④ 重庆大学

　　孟北京在 B 城一家袜厂上班。这袜厂规模很小，也就是三十几个工人，但它有个响亮的名字：前进。前进袜厂几十年如一日地生产一种"前进"牌线袜，这种袜子穿在脚上透气性能还好，可是你一开始走路它就开始前进，它随着你的步伐，慢慢从脚腕儿退至脚后跟，再退至脚心最终堆积至脚尖。或者，它也可能在你的脚上旋转，平白无故的，这袜子的后跟就会转到你的脚面上来。如若这时你恰好当众抬起了你的脚，谁都会看见你的脚面上正"趴"着一只脚后跟。这可像个什么样子啊，它呈现出的怪异和滑稽，就好比你突然发现某个人的后脑勺上正努着一副嘴唇。

　　本世纪 70 年代初，孟北京刚进厂时就穿自己厂里织出的这种袜子，到了 90 年代末，那些和孟北京一块儿进厂的工人，"奔儿头"小林子李二香他们早就不穿这"前进"牌了，这线袜却依然在孟北京的脚上前进或者旋转。倒不是说孟北京格外喜欢自己厂里的产品，他一点儿也不喜欢，可是他习惯了，习惯成自然。此外，还有一个原因大约是他的经济状况。他的经济十分拮据，前进牌线袜不能说"物美"，但是"价廉"。

　　有一次他在公共汽车上看见一个男人的脚，一眼便认出那人脚上穿的就是他们厂的袜子：后跟已然扭到了脚面上，耸起皱皱巴巴的鼓包儿。这发现使孟北京感到亲切心安，他多想伸出自己的脚与那男人的并在一起，然后对他说：你瞧瞧你瞧瞧，咱们是同类啊，咱们是一种人。孟北京自信，能在 90 年代末期坚持穿前进牌袜子的人与他定是一个阶层，并且在生活的某个方面与他定有着同一种主张。他很希望能有确凿的事实，用看得见摸得着的依据来证明他的不孤立，他的从属于某个群体。

翻译区：_____

_____

_____

_____

_____

_____

_____

_____

_____

_____

_____

_____

5 扬州大学

中国特色社会主义进入新时代，我国社会主要矛盾已经转化为人民日益增长的美好生活需要和不平衡不充分的发展之间的矛盾。必须认识到，我国社会主要矛盾的变化是关系全局的历史性变化，对党和国家工作提出了许多新要求。

必须认识到，我国社会主要矛盾的变化，没有改变我们对我国社会主义所处历史阶段的判断，我国仍处于并将长期处于社会主义初级阶段的基本国情没有变，我国是世界最大发展中的国际地位没有变。

翻译区：_____

_____

_____

_____

_____

_____

_____

_____

_____

_____

_____

_____

_____

_____

_____

_____

_____

_____

6 华东理工大学

　　人类从历史一开始就不断进行实证观察，但其影响常常十分有限。毕竟，如果我们觉得已经有了所有问题的答案，为什么还要浪费资源进行新的观察？然而，现代人们开始承认自己在某些非常重要的问题上几近无知，就开始觉得需要寻找取得全新的知识。因此，主流的现代研究方法就会预设旧知识有所不足。而且，这时候的重点不在于研究旧的知识体系，而是要强调新的观测、新的实验。如果现在观察到的现象与过去的传统知识体系相冲突，我们会认为现在的观察才正确。当然，如果是研究宇宙星系的物理学家、研究青铜时期城市的考古学家或是研究资本主义产生的政治学家，就不会忽略传统知识体系。他们会研究过去的智者究竟写了什么、说了什么。

翻译区：

7 北京师范大学

这是两年前的事。五月端阳，渡船头祖父找人作了代替，便带了黄狗同翠翠进城，到大河边去看划船。河边站满了人，四只朱色长船在潭中滑着，龙船水刚刚涨过，河中水皆豆绿色，天气又那么明朗，鼓声蓬蓬响着，翠翠抿着嘴一句话不说，心中充满了不可言说的快乐。河边人太多了一点，各人皆尽张着眼睛望河中，不多久，黄狗还留在身边，祖父却挤得不见了。

先是两人同黄狗进城前一天，祖父就问翠翠："明天城里划船，倘若一个人去看，人多怕不怕？"翠翠就说："人多我不怕，但自己只是一个人可不好玩。"于是祖父想了半天，方想起一个住在城中的老熟人，赶夜里到城里去商量，请那老人来看一天渡船，自己却陪翠翠进城玩一天。到了河边后，长潭里的四只红船，把翠翠的注意力完全占去了，身边祖父似乎也可有可无了。祖父心想："时间还早，到收场时，至少还得三个时刻。溪边的那个朋友，也应当来看看年青人的热闹，回去一趟，换换地位还赶得及。"因此就告翠翠，"人太多了，站在这里看，不要动，我到别处去有点事情，无论如何总赶得回来伴你回家。"翠翠正为两只竞速并进的船迷着，祖父说的话毫不思索就答应了。祖父知道黄狗在翠翠身边，也许比他自己在她身边还稳当，于是便回家看船去了。

翻译区：

_____

_____

_____

_____

_____

_____

_____

_____

_____

_____

_____

_____

_____

_____

_____

_____

8 武汉大学

书房永远是令人向往的去处。

我从事笔耕数十年，从来没有一间自己的书房，一间独立的、完整的、名副其实的书房。我多次迁居，从大城市直至外省人烟稀少的小山村。每次搬家时，唯有书籍最累人，也最难舍弃。

我爱书，说不上藏书丰富，日积月累倒也可观，几经迁移，不但没有损失，反而日益增多，因为居处的局限，每每有书满为患之感。现在我的卧室就是书房，群书延伸到小卫生间的大书架上，无法腾出一室作书房。

然而，在我的文学生涯中，一度也有一间自己的书房。所谓"书房"，其实是一间贮藏室。那幢在本世纪初期落成的陈旧宅第，开间很大，楼下一间屋子就可作为街道办的托儿所。我的一家住在三楼一大间，按今日标准，至少可分成三间，真是大而无当。不过房门外，紧靠楼梯，有一间贮藏室，倒是极为难得的。门一关，可与全家的生活区完全隔绝，避免尚在幼年的孩子们往来干扰。

这贮藏室于是成了我一生中唯一的书房，也许称之为"小作坊"更为贴切。狭长逼仄的一小间，北窗下靠墙置一旧书桌，进门处兀立两只叠起来的玻璃书柜，都是原先住户废弃的家具。除了窗下书桌前可容纳我的一把旧藤椅，就没有多余的空间了。不过，这样的一间书房，一个人躲在里面写作，思想很集中。

翻译区：_____

_____

_____

_____

_____

_____

_____

_____

_____

_____

_____

_____

_____

_____

⑨ 中南大学

中国哲学家们的社会经济思想都强调要区别"本"和"末"，农业生产被认为是立国之本，而商业则被看为是立国之末端，因为经济生产主要靠农业，而商业只关系到产品的交换。商品的交换终究要以生产为前提，在一个以农业为基础的国家里，农产品是主要的产品，因此在中国历史上，各种社会、经济的理论和政策都重农抑商。

在一个重农轻商的国家里，商人自不免受到轻视。在中国的传统社会里，把民众按行业分为士、农、工、商四等，士通常是来自地主阶级，农就是从事农业生产的农民，这两种行业受到社会的尊重，任何人出身于"耕读世家"，往往引以为傲。

读书人通常并不亲自耕地，但他们一般出身于地主家庭，家庭的兴衰和农业生产的好坏直接联系在一起；农业收成好，他们受益；农业收成坏，他们也受连累。因此，他们的宇宙观和人生观主要反映了农民的思想。再加上他们受过教育，使他们得以表达农民自己没法表达的思想，这种表达在中国就采取了哲学、文学和艺术的形式。

翻译区：_____

_____

_____

_____

_____

_____

_____

_____

_____

_____

_____

_____

_____

_____

_____

_____

_____

_____

_____

⑩ 西南大学

中国哲学的历史中有个主流，可以叫做中国哲学的精神。为了解这个精神，我们需要首先弄清楚绝大多数中国哲学家力求解决的问题。

人是各式各样的，每一种人都可以取得最高的成就。例如，有的人从政，在这个领域里，最高成就便是成为一个伟大的政治家。同样，在艺术领域里，最高成就便是成为一个伟大的艺术家。人可能被分为不同等级，但他们都是人。就做人来说，最高成就是什么呢？按中国哲学说，就是成圣，成圣的最高成就是：个人与宇宙合而为一。问题在于，如果人追求天人合一，是否需要抛弃社会，甚至否定人生呢？

有的哲学家认为，必须如此。释迦牟尼认为，人生就是苦难的根源；柏拉图认为，身体是灵魂的监狱；道家有人认为，生命是个赘疣，是个瘤。所有这些看法都主张人应该从被物质败坏了的世界中解脱出来。一个圣人要想取得最高的成就，必须抛弃社会。唯有这样，才能得到最后的解脱。这种哲学通常被称为"出世"的哲学。

还有一种哲学，强调社会中的人际关系和人事。这种哲学只谈道德价值，因此对于超越道德的价值觉得无从谈起，也不愿去探讨。这种哲学通常被称为"入世"的哲学。站在入世哲学的立场上，出世哲学过于理想化，不切实际，因而是消极的。从出世哲学的立场看，入世哲学过于实际，也因而过于肤浅；它诚然积极，但是像一个走错了路的人，走得越快，在歧途上就走得越远。

翻译区：_____

_____

_____

_____

_____

_____

_____

_____

_____

_____

_____

_____

_____

◆◆◆ **参考译文 10 篇** ◆◆◆

① 天津大学

Education and schools are the last to be neglected. Australia, an unpopulous country in southern hemisphere, has put education first ever since its founding. It is the first country to build Air School and sets a model for other countries. Australia has a population of 21.7 million and most of them live in the southeastern areas and several big coastal cities in the north. In the vast inland and remotes areas, however, are scattered only natives and a small number of people who work in animal husbandry, mining and railway transportation. Most of them live away from cities and towns. As a result, Air School, designed to meet the needs of those who can't go to school due to illnesses, disability or remoteness, comes into existence.

In our country, there was Horseback School in the liberated areas in war times. Today, Australia, by means of modern technologies, creates Air School which is very popular among local children. Compared with other developed countries, it is a late-starter but a universally acknowledged developed country. Its economy ranks high in the world only within decades and its people are inventive and creative. Australia is also famous for its environment-friendliness and education. Air School is the first of its kind. (罗国强 译)

② 华中师范大学

The couple live among Shanghai citizens and are surely influenced by their ways of life, like saving money for future use. They are mainly interested is in eating and most of their salaries are spent on food. They have a good appetite and are willing to spend money on food; however, they, in the eyes of their grandma, are not discriminating in food choices. For example, they dine out every two or three days, but at fixed restaurants, like Fuxing Western Food and Lvye Chuanyang Restaurants across the street; a little far away are SUNYA Cantonese Restaurant and Hongchangxing Mutton House on Nanjing Road. It doesn't mean that these restaurants are not good, but they are hardly discriminating and only attracted by reputations of the restaurants. They dine in the same restaurants again and again and most of the dishes they prefer are the same few, heavy-flavored and large-portioned. This habit of eating meat dishes was probably developed when they were in the troops.

Their grandma is good at cooking Yangzhou cuisine. It well fits and also enhances their taste. The fully cooked, flavor-soaked and dark reddish Yangzhou cuisine requires fine work, fine ingredients and slow cooking. The dishes cooked by their grandmother exhibit a more rural style, featuring a stronger taste and a particularly generous use of soy sauce. Though not so delicate, they are the most delicious food to them. Therefore, they often hold gatherings at home to entertain their friends. All guests admire the cooking of their grandma. They have many friends. And more or less influenced by their army life, they are forthright and enthusiastic. When their friends come, they ask them to sit down and eat, not caring about formal manners. They hold gatherings every three or five days, living a cheerful life. (罗国强 译)

③ 北京林业大学

At present, the chronic contradictions accumulated in the rapid growth of petrochemical industry have become increasingly apparent. The growth model is relatively extensive, the structural contradictions are prominent, the industry is large in economic scale but not strong and there are increasing constraints from resources and the environment. Since the second half of last year, the international financial crisis has made quite an impact on the petrochemical industry. Therefore, it is urgent to improve the overall quality of the industry and increase market competitiveness through structural adjustment and industrial upgrading.

The structural imbalance is acute for our petrochemical industry. Petrochemical products, organic chemical products and new high-end products make up quite a small percentage while high-consumption, roughly-processed or low value-added products, by contrast, account for a high percentage. We should innovate technologically, developing advanced manufacturing and processing technologies for new products; we should extend the industrial chain and diversify products; and we should make high-performance products and make specialized, green and high value-added products. Only by doing these things can we optimize product mix, increase industrial competitiveness and improve the supporting capacity for other relevant industries in our country. (罗国强 译)

④ 重庆大学

Meng Beijing works in a sock factory in city B. The factory is quite small with only 30-odd workers, but its name sounds ambitious and impressive, "Advance". The factory has been producing Advance-brand socks for several decades. The socks are fairly breathable, but when you walk, they slip slowly from your ankle to heel with your step and then to the middle of your feet and ultimately to your tiptoe. Or they may revolve, their rear bottom part, imperceptibly, revolving to your upper feet. After that, if you happen to raise your foot before others, they will be surprised to see the lower side of your sock on your upper foot. What an embarrassing thing! It is so weird and funny as if you saw an open mouth on the back of a head.

Meng wore this kind of socks when he entered the factory in the early 1970s. By the late 1990s, several of his co-workers who entered the factory in the same year had long since abandoned the socks. But Meng didn't give up. It wasn't that he had particular favor to them. Actually, he didn't like the brand at all. Then why? He got accustomed to it. Another reason may be that he led a poor life. The Advance socks were cheap, though not good in quality.

One day he happened to see a man's feet in a bus and recognized the socks that man was wearing were exactly made by his factory. The rear bottoms of the socks had rolled to that man's upper feet, wrinkled. It made Meng feel warm and relieved. How eager he was to stand next to the man, showing his socks and saying "Look! We wear the same socks. We are the same." He firmly believed that those who wore the socks until the late 1990s must have belonged to his class, and shared the same idea in some aspects of life. He wished to get some hard facts and concrete evidence to prove that he was not alone and indeed belonged to a certain group.（罗国强 译）

⑤ 扬州大学

As China has entered a new era of building socialism with Chinese characteristics, the major social contradiction has shifted to one between the ever-growing need for a better life and unbalanced and inadequate development. We must realize that the evolution is a historic change concerning the overall situation, bringing many new requirements for the work of both the Party and the country.

We must also realize the evolution doesn't change our judgement of the historical stage where China's socialism stands. The basic reality hasn't been changed that China is still in the primary stage of socialism and will last for a long time, which remains the largest developing country in the world.（罗国强 译）

⑥ 华东理工大学

Human beings have been making empirical observations since the beginning of history, but its influence has often been limited. After all, if we thought we had found out the answers to all the questions, why do we expend resources on further observations? Modern people, however, begin to admit that they are almost ignorant of some very important issues, thus finding it necessary to explore and learn entirely new knowledge. Therefore, the mainstream modern research methods will presuppose that the old knowledge is insufficient. And the research focus now is on new observations and new experiments rather than on the old knowledge system. If the observed phenomenon runs into conflict with the old knowledge, we believe the newly acquired knowledge is right. Of course, a physicist studying cosmic galaxy, an archaeologist studying cities during the Bronze Age or a political scientist studying the origin of capitalism, won't ignore the traditional knowledge system. Instead, they will study what the wise men wrote or said in the past.（罗国强 译）

⑦ 北京师范大学

Two years before this, on the fifth of the fifth month, her grandfather found someone to mind the ferry while he took Brownie and Emerald into town to watch the dragon-boat race. The bank was thick with people as four long vermilion boats came rowing upstream. The river had just begun to rise and in the sunlight the water was pea-green. As the drums rolled, Emerald bit her lips, happier than words could tell. So many eager spectators were milling round that she did not notice when her grandfather disappeared, leaving her with Brownie.

The day before he had asked: "If you went alone to see the boat race tomorrow, would you be afraid of the crowds?" "No, I wouldn't," she said. "But it's no fun all alone." At that he bethought himself of an old friend in town and went in that same night to ask him to see to the ferry for one day, so that he could give Emerald a good time. Once by the river, the boats claimed all her attention. The ferryman thought, "There's still a good three or four hours to go. My friend oughtn't to miss this. I'll go back and change with him." He told Emerald, "There's such a mob here, don't move away. I've something to do, but I'll be back for sure to take you home." Intent on two boats now abreast, she agreed without thinking. And knowing that Brownie would guard her, the old man left. （杨宪益、戴乃迭 译）

8 武汉大学

A study is always a place of enormous appeal to us.

I've been engaged in writing for several decades, but I've never had a study of my own — a study that is independent, intact and true to its name, that is. I've moved many times, once even away from a big city to a remote small mountain village in another province. Whenever I moved, my books, cumbersome as they were, turned out to be the last thing for me to part with.

I'm a bibliophile. My collection of books is far from being a big private library, but it keeps growing from day to day. Several times of house moving did not disperse my collection. On the contrary, it has become larger with each passing day until my small dwelling is overcrowded with them. Now the shelves of books in my study-cum-bedroom extend as far as the tiny toilet. No room is available to serve specifically as a study.

However, in the course of my career as a writer, I did once own a study, or, to be exact, a storeroom turned study. I was then living in an old house built at the turn of the century. It was quite roomy, so much so that the ground floor served even as a neighborhood nursery. I and family lived in a room on the third floor, which was really big but impractical because, according to today's standard, it could have been divided into at least three rooms. Fortunately, close to the staircase just outside my room, there was a storeroom, which I regarded as something of great rarity to me because sitting inside it behind the closed door I could cut myself off from my family and work without any disturbance from my small kids.

The storeroom was the only study I've ever had in my life. Perhaps it could be aptly called a workshop. It was long, narrow and small. An old desk stood against a wall under the northern window. Two piled-up glass bookcases rose erect near the entrance. They were the furniture abandoned by a former resident. There was no room for anything else besides my old cane chair placed before the desk under the window. However, enjoying the privacy of a so-called study like this, I could do writing with high concentration. （张培基 译）

⑨　中南大学

In the social and economic thinking of Chinese philosophers, there is a distinction between what they call "the root" and "the branch". "The root" refers to agriculture and "the branch" to commerce. The reason for this is that agriculture is concerned with production, while commerce is merely concerned with exchange. One must have production before one can have exchange. In an agrarian country, agriculture is the major form of production, and therefore throughout Chinese history, social and economic theories and policies have all attempted "to emphasize the root and slight the branch".

The people who deal with the "branch", that is, the merchants, were therefore looked down upon. They were the last and lowest of the four traditional classes of society, the other three being scholars, farmers, and artisans. The scholars were usually landlords, and the farmers were the peasants who actually cultivated the land. These were the two honorable professions in China. A family having "a tradition of studying and farming" was something of which to be proud.

Although the "scholars" did not actually cultivate the land themselves, yet since they were usually landlords, their fortunes were tied up with agriculture. A good or bad harvest meant their good or bad fortune, and therefore their reaction to the universe and their outlook on life were essentially those of the farmer. In addition, their education gave them the power to express what an actual farmer felt but was incapable of expressing himself. This expression took the form of Chinese philosophy, literature, and art.

（冯友兰：《中国哲学简史》，外语教学与研究出版社 2000 年版）

⑩　西南大学

In the history of Chinese philosophy there is a mainstream—the spirit of Chinese philosophy. To understand the spirit, we should first make clear the problem that most Chinese philosophers have tried to solve.

Humans are diverse and they each can make the greatest achievement in a certain field. For example, becoming a great statesman is the greatest achievement for those who engage in politics and becoming a great artist is the biggest achievement for those working in the field of art. Humans may belong to different classes, but they have one thing in common: they are humans. Then what is the greatest achievement when they are solely a human? According to Chinese philosophy, it is to be a sage whose greatest achievement is to get integrated into the universe. But the question is whether they should abandon society and even deny life in order to pursue the goal.

The answer for some philosophers is absolutely "yes". Siddhartha says life is the root of suffering; Plato believes that human body is the prison of soul; some Taoists argue that life is a tumor, useless and superfluous. All of them hold that we should be freed from the material-corrupted world. A sage, if he wants to make the most outstanding achievement, has to leave society. Only in this way can he get final extrication. Such a philosophy is called "supermundane" philosophy.

There is another philosophy emphasizing interpersonal relationships and human behaviors in society. This one, often called "mundane" philosophy, only discusses moral values, and anything beyond morality is hardly to be explored. From the perspective of the mundane philosophy, the supermundane philosophy is too ideal, unrealistic and thus negative. Meanwhile, the mundane philosophy, in the eyes of the supermundane philosophy, is too pragmatic and too superficial; it, though literally active, is like someone to have walked on a wrong road. The faster he walks, the farther he will go in the wrong direction. （罗国强 译）

附二：参考文献

［1］冯庆华：《英汉翻译基础教程》，高等教育出版社 2008 年版，第 13 页。

［2］冯庆华、陈科芳：《汉英翻译基础教程》，高等教育出版社 2008 年版，第 48~49、52~53、101~106、117~120 页。

［3］李长栓：《非文学翻译理论与实践》，中译出版社 2012 年版，第 18~32、140~144 页。

［4］李长栓、施晓菁：《理解与表达—汉英翻译案例讲评》，外文出版社 2012 年版，第 166~171、241~243、247~254 页。

［5］王友贵："意识形态与 20 世纪中国文学翻译史"，载《中国翻译》2003 年第 5 期。

［6］章振邦：《新编英语语法教程》，上海外语教育出版社 2013 年版，第 476 页。

［7］Joan Pinkham、姜桂华：《中式英语之鉴》，外语教学与研究出版社 2000 年版，第 3~13 页。